Living Faith
Went To Cuba

Living Faith Went To Cuba

Makes God Real

E. FAITH STEWART

To order additional copies of this book, contact:
Xlibris LLC
1-888-795-4274
www.Xlibris.com
Orders@Xlibris.com
142938

CONTENTS

Dedication

I humbly dedicate this little volume to the YOUNG MINISTRY of the church today, with an earnest prayer that God may help each of you to catch a vision of God's greatness and of His power, and also of your responsibility in lifting high the standard of His Word of Promise. A "Living Faith" in God and in His Word can only be maintained in the earth as long as the Ministry—both by example and by teaching keeps the TRUTH before the people. While God lets me live my prayer for you shall be that the Holy Fire of a "Living Faith" may be kept burning in your hearts. Amen.

E. Faith Stewart

SOME OF E. FAITH STEWARTS CHILDREN IN CUBA

FLORIDA DEC. 1954

FOREWORD

It has been my privilege to spend about thirty-three years in Foreign Missionary Work, besides a goodly number of years in both pastoral and evangelistic work in the United States and the British Isles. Most of this time, I have lived and laboured without any definite means of support, but trusting alone in God to supply all my personal needs and the needs of the work to which He had called me. Some of our experiences have been marvelous indeed. Yes, too marvelous to keep hidden away from the heart of the Church in these perilous days in which we are now living, when every Christian needs all the encouragement to their faith that it is possible to have. True Christian people everywhere are suffering things the world did not dream of before. They all need all the spiritual nourishment they can get to build them up in the most holy faith, and to make them able to stand against the wiles of the devil in these days of apostasy. Today we hear men who hold high positions in the nominal Christian world, and even some who at one time were looked up to by the Church as real rocks for God and Truth, scoffing at the sincere testimony of "answered prayer" and unhesitatingly they put the miracle working power of the Son of God as something definitely of the past. For instance, the healing of the body of physical affliction in answer to the prayer of faith, is unhesitatingly set aside. They laugh to scorn at the very suggestion of taking the temporal cares of life before the throne of God in prayer, with the hope of having divine intervention in these things. Most of the Books of Prayer that have been published are so deeply intellectual and so lacking in the divine unction that absolutely no inspiration comes to the soul through reading them. As I have beheld these conditions my heart has cried out to God to help us in some way to lift up before the world, and to preserve the Bible Standard of Active Living Faith in our LIVING GOD and in HIS DIVINE PROMISES.

For years past I have been urged by ministerial brethren to write a book on "answers to prayer;" but I have definitely believed it would not be accepted by many, and for this reason I hesitated. Seeing the powers of unbelief increasing, and the hearts of God's true people just crying out for something that will lift up their faith to a higher plane, I have decided to frankly write this book of testimonies of **what God is doing today.** I send it out with the hope that many souls may be inspired and lifted up to a higher plane of faith and a deeper depth of obedience to God through reading it. To this end, I pray sincerely that the dear Lord will add His blessings to this feeble effort. If this is accomplished, my efforts will have been well rewarded.

As you read, meditate on the following questions—Whose God are you serving? A God that has ears but that hears not? A God that has eyes but they see not the sufferings of His people? A God that has hands but they are never out-stretched to administer help to those who have need? What God are you serving? Bless the Lord, I am serving the God of Isaac, of Abraham, and of Jacob. I am serving the very same God who quenched the fire in the heated furnace and delivered the three Hebrew boys. I am serving the Living Christ of God who was first seen as He walked in the midst of the fire with the Hebrew boys while they were in the furnace, "and the form of the fourth was like unto the Son of God" Daniel 3:19-25. Glory be to God, He is still walking in the midst of the furnace of affliction or sufferings right by the side of His followers, to DELIVER THEM. Yes, my God is the God of Daniel, and He can still close the mouth of lions when they rise up to destroy God's people. WHAT A MIGHTY GOD WE DO SERVE! My God is the God of all earth and heaven. He metes the mighty waters of the seas in His hand— and THAT HAND upholds me—yes, it upholds all of God's trusting people today. Bless the Lord, oh my soul and ALL that is within me, bless HIS HOLY NAME forever.

Do you feel, troubled soul, that you are sinking—sinking to rise no more? Just lift up your eyes as did Peter and cry out from your heart, and those GREAT OMNIPOTENT arms of God will encircle you and carry you safely through. I KNOW IN WHOM I HAVE BELIEVED, and I know that He is able. This book goes forth with a prayer that it may accomplish just what God has purposed to accomplish through its message—Amen.

E. FAITH STEWART.

The workers receive a new family of children

CHAPTER I

"Have Faith In God"—Mark 11:22

If anyone were to ask me what I consider the basic stone in the foundation of victorious Christian living, or in the successful activities in Christian work, I would unhesitatingly answer—*Living faith in God and His word of promise.* One may have a sincere heart; a willingness to sacrifice for the cause; a loving disposition; devotion to their religion; one may be very honest and upright in all their dealings with mankind. All these qualities are very good. They are all absolutely necessary in the Christian life, but still with any of these or with all of them together, the Christian life is still lacking greatly if not actually unctionized and kept in action by the *power of faith.* I fear that the people, so few in number, who realize the value of definite living faith in the Lord, are the only true Christians living. You may ask almost anyone if they have faith in God, and the answer will be in the affirmative. But do they really have faith in Him? Do they believe His Word? Do they live by it?

To have faith in God, one must definitely have faith in His divine plan that covers the needs of this life and of the life to come. One must have absolute confidence in His word of promise, and if we do have this faith it will work mighty things in our individual lives. And the working out of these things will make our lives resplendent with the Light of the Gospel of Christ. God is so mighty and His promises are so very powerful (and dependable) that active faith naturally brings results. Just as surely as His spoken word brought light, and even separated light from darkness, thus making day and night; just as surely as Christ's spoken word calmed the raging seas or healed the leper; or as truly as His word of blessing over the loaves and fishes caused them to be multiplied until the hungry multitude were fed with an abundance; just so His written word of promise carries with it today something of His divine self—bringing into the very lives of the faithful believers a power that surpasses all else the world has ever known. And the world today is surely in need of clear demonstration of this kind of power.

We are living in an age where the fruits of active faith are scarcely seen in the lives of Christians. Many are living so far below their privileges as children of God that the world looking on, sees nothing attractive in the religion of Jesus Christ. And this same formal worship; this same fruitless, joyless profession is the very basis of the increasing infidelity we see all around us in the world today. How is the world going to believe in the Gospel if they see no fulfillment of the promises of God, in the lives of those who profess to be His? May the dear Lord, by the power of His spirit, awaken Christian brethren everywhere to a realization of their responsibility in keeping up the true standard of confidence in the divine power of the Gospel.

We are living in an age of infidelity, and daily the powers of unbelief are increasing more and more. Nearly all schools of higher learning are literally filled with professors who are filling the minds of the noble youth of the land with false teachings that undermine all their confidence in God and in the Divinity of Christ, and in His miracle working power. Communism, infidelity, and atheism are filling the popular schools of learning and turning the world away from the Saviour; and what are we doing while all this is going on? Are we doing our part to lift up the standard of the Bible? Jesus Christ came first of all as the Saviour of our souls; but He has also come as the healer of our bodies. He came as the mighty miracle working Christ of God, and bless the dear Lord, the day of miracles *is not* past. Do not the sacred scriptures declare Him to be the unchanging Christ? "Jesus Christ, the same yesterday, and today and forever" Heb. 13:8. Yes, thank God, they do, and to those of us who have refused to lower the standard of the Gospel, this declaration "Jesus Christ the same—," has become a living reality in our lives. Praise the Lord forever!

When Jesus Christ was on earth, walking the shores of Galilee, and going in and out among the people, healing *all manner* of sicknesses and diseases, casting out demons, opening the eyes of the blind, causing the lame to walk, multiplying the food to satisfy the hunger of the great multitude, His heart was saddened at seeing the little faith His own disciples had in the power of His word. Walking along the roadside with some of them one day, and seeing a fig tree without any fruit on it, He (Christ) said unto it (the tree) "No man eat fruit of thee hereafter forever" Mark 11:14. (The disciples had heard Him.) The following day they returned over the same road and seeing the fig tree dried up from the roots, one of them in amazement called the Master's attention to the tree and its withered condition. In sadness the Master replied saying, "Have faith in God" Mark 11:22. Just following this incident, a man went to Jesus complaining that he had taken his son, possessed with a dumb spirit to some of the disciples asking them to cast out the spirit, and that they failed to do it. Jesus then cast out the dumb spirit from the boy and then He reproved His disciples saying unto them, "Oh faithless generation; how long shall I be with you" Mark 9:17-27. When the disciples saw the deliverance of this boy they turned to Jesus with troubled hearts asking Him why they had failed, and He replied saying to them, "This kind goeth not out but by *Fasting* and *prayer."* These words of our Heavenly Father convey to us a deep message of divine *Truth*. Fasting and prayer many times accomplishes what prayer alone cannot do. Fasting does not increase God's power or His willingness; but it does bring the seeker into a depth of earnestness before God, that is many times lacking in prayer alone. The act of self-denial manifested in sincere fasting while presenting a burden before the Lord prepares our hearts and brings us into closer relationship with the Lord. It enables us to stand definitely on the promises of God, *expecting the answer.* Fasting in prayer by individuals or by congregations is today almost a forgotten *service to God.* If it were necessary for Jesus to fast that He might have power and victory over the power of the devil, how much more necessary for us today. If it were necessary for Christ to so deeply feel the burden of responsibility that was falling on Him—the Son of God—that He was carried off alone in fasting and prayer until His soul was saturated with the divine power of His Father; and He (Jesus) was strengthened to finish the work the Father had given Him to do in His great redemption plan, how much more necessary it must be for us to keep so definitely in touch with His will that all He has purposed to be accomplished through His Church may be demonstrated before the unbelieving world through His children today. The world is full of infidelity today because the professed people of God have so lowered the standard of the Word that all they have to offer suffering Humanity is a powerless message. If Christ were to open His lips in these days to reprove the unbelieving professors, as He did in that day when he was walking with some of His disciples along the country road, when He finally, out of a burdened heart said, "Have faith in God", I wonder what He would now say? May God put a Holy burden in each of our hearts until we, as His chosen people, rise up to defend the glorious Gospel in its fullness and power. Shortly after the incident referred to, Christ again tried to draw His children into a place where they could be strong enough to withstand the power of darkness in the evil days that were coming upon the earth. He pointed out God's faithfulness to those who call on Him in faith—but He was able to see the great Apostasy coming in on the Church and saw the day approaching when men just would "not endure sound doctrine", and would lose their faith in God's power and in His Written Word. He cried out of a burdened heart "when the Son of man cometh, will He find faith on the earth?" Luke 18:8. This sad expression, wrung from the very heart of our Lord Jesus, should awaken every true child of God; putting in each of their hearts, the decision to so live that their own faith be not hindered, and that they be determined that their own lives be a clear example and a definite demonstration of what can be done through prayer and faith. One thing that many times hinders the prayer of faith is having brethren who are weak in the faith, and who do not trust God for their own healing, come forward and lay on hands for the healing of others. God's Word says in 2 Tim. 2:6 "The husbandman that laboureth, must be first partaker of the fruits. Consider what I say and the Lord give thee understanding in all things." Oh, how very necessary it is for us to really understand spiritual things. How can one pray for the definite healing of another if they do not pray the prayer of faith; or if they do not believe enough to trust God to heal their own bodies? We must be living examples of unwavering faith in the unchanging promises of the Father's Written Word, if we are to be an inspiration and encouragement to our brethren.

God's Word not only contains promises of healing, but it contains definite promises that actually cover every phrase of life—the spiritual, the physical, and the temporal. God promises to *keep* by His grace; to *guide* by His spirit; to *comfort* and *strengthen*; yes, He promises to *heal* by His virtue. In few words He has promised to be to us always "a very present help in the time of need" Ps. 46:1. If we live where we are on believing grounds, He will be to us everything we have need of. Believing ground—"If ye abide in me, and my words abide in you (then) ye shall ask what ye will, and it shall be done unto you." John 15:7. Brother, do you believe this? Is it a definite reality in your life? We read again in Acts

17:28 "For in Him we live and move and have our being." Praise God. I ask again—is this experience a blessed reality in your own life? If you must answer *no* to these questions, then may I ask—what is Christ to you? If He is not your present help in trouble, your deliverer, your healer, your guide—your all and in all—then what is He to you? If you know nothing of that close intimate relation between you and the Lord Jesus, that just makes the promises a living reality, then what are you getting out of the Christian life?

May God so move on the heart of His great Church that once more in the "Evening of Time" we may see many mighty works being done, and many mighty signs following as was seen in the Morning time of the Gospel Age. We all believe He worked in mighty power in the Church in the Morning Time. But what about these days? Why not now? God is *unchanging,* His word is *forever settled in heaven.* Creeds of men may change. Laws of men that govern any and everything that pertains to this world may, and do change—but the laws of God including His commandments and plans that govern the spiritual life as well as His promises are unchanging. Weary Christian, lift up your eyes unto the Lord from whence cometh your help, and draw nigh unto Him, seeking divine help until you personally reach that place of restful confidence that will bring an end to your struggles. Every promise He has made should be as a land-mark for our faith.

What is your need? Healing of the body? If you are living for His own glory, then it is *His will* to heal you. Read III John 2, "Beloved, I wish above all things, that thou mayest prosper and be in health, even as thy soul prospers." Read this over and over, and meditate on it. Open up your heart and drink it in. This statement was made for you. Reach up and make it your own. Let your soul expand as you meditate on God's marvelous love and your faith *must* enlarge until the first thing you know you will be crying out from the depth of your soul, "Yes, Lord I do believe, I do believe!" The only answer there ever will be to the question asked by our Lord Jesus—in Luke 18:8, "When the Son of man cometh will He find faith on the earth?"—*must come from the ones who truly represent Him here in the faith.* What will your answer to this question be? What will my answer be? There will only be "faith on earth" at that last great day *If His True Children* maintain their individual faith alive and active to the end of their sojourn below. In so doing, they will then have enriched the world and the Church by faith in Him; and by their example and at their departure for the heavenly home, will leave behind them seeds of gospel truth that will be eternal. Before closing this chapter, let me ask the reader—what are you individually doing by your life and testimony and teaching to preserve to the end the true Bible standard of faith in God and in His Word? Let us develop by God's help to where we shall be living examples of the believers—true disciples of our Saviour—Jesus Christ. "Have faith in God," and preserve it.

CHAPTER II

"Faith Cometh By Hearing" (Or Reading)

That "faith cometh by hearing—and hearing by the Word" is true, and today there is a great famine in the world—and this famine is caused by a lack of the knowledge of God's full plan for the care of His children. One thing that ought to be convincing is a statement made in I Cor. 6:19-20. It reads thus, *"What? know ye not that your body is the temple of the Holy Ghost which is in you, which ye have of God, and ye are not your own? For ye are bought with a price (even the precious blood of Christ) therefore, glorify God in your body, and in your spirit, which are His."* Yes, if we are His children, we have been bought by Christ's sacrifice—both soul and body. Then knowing that we have been bought definitely, and that He owns us, should we not be able to believe that He wants to care for us, both soul and body. Yes, His plan covers all, and if we can grasp this *truth,* it will be a stay to us all along life's pathway.

The lack of knowledge of God's full plan for us is the basic cause for the unbelief there is in the world today. The ministers of the gospel of Christ are responsible for much of the lack of faith in the love and power of God today. And my earnest prayer is that the dear Lord may awaken His true ministers to a very definite realization of their responsibility, and that there may be a mighty revival of the old time confidence and faith in the Promises of God. And to those of God's dear children who are not where they can have their faith built up by the preaching of God's Word on these lines, I am happy to say that you are not left without hope—for thank God, we still have today the privilege of searching the Scriptures for ourselves. By thus searching out God's divine plan, and His promises for ourselves, we may build up our own souls in the most holy faith, and keep the fire of faith burning within our hearts daily. In the Bible we have an abundance of examples of what God has done in ages past for those who have trusted Him, and if we do believe that He is just the same today—and will be the same forever, then we need not go on suffering for the lack of His divine care, whether that is to be manifested in the healing of our bodies, or the supply of our temporal needs, or His divine protection, or His guidance in all the various conditions of life.

In Acts 17:11, we read of some who were counted more noble than others in that they searched the Scriptures daily to find out if the things they heard reported were true. They believed the Scriptures and took time daily to search out the great *truths* of God for themselves. And it is true today that anyone who will do the same thing, will be convinced of the *Truth,* and will be built up in the faith, and be able to see marvelous things done in the name of the Holy Child Jesus. We only need to exercise faith in the Promises of God and we shall receive. But since the promises of God are *Conditional*—we need to carefully study the condition of each promise and then see to it that we do meet these conditions, and *then* faith will become active and will take hold of God and get the answer.

In James 5:16 we read, "Confess your faults one to another, that you may be healed." If there is ought in our lives that does not please God, we *must* do our part to remove this—to get it out of the way, and then prayer can be effective. Sometimes confession only needs to be made to God, but there are times when we need to clear something out of the way that hinders the confidence of others, and this can only be done by confessing to the person concerned.

If there has been carelessness in our life in any way, or slackness In our devotional life this must be definitely settled between us and God and if we want His divine healing touch on our bodies, or His help in other ways. In John 15:7 we read, "If ye abide in me, and my words abide in you (then) ye shall ask what ye will, and *it shall be done unto you.*" The *condition*—definitely abiding in the Lord, just living a settled, solid life for His Glory.

In James 4:3 we read, "Ye ask, and receive not, *because* ye ask amiss, that ye may consume it upon your own lusts." Selfish praying does not bring us in touch with the throne of God, and therefore does not bring the answer down. What is the object of your desire to have prayer answered? That God may be glorified? That Christ may be exalted? Is it that the cause of Christ and His Gospel may be advanced? Do you want to be healed so you can enjoy the pleasures of the world, or so you may serve the Lord Jesus better? Let us examine well our motives in coming to the Lord for His help, and then with pure hearts and right desires let us approach Him in faith to receive *all* He has promised in His Holy Word. May God bless and inspire active faith in each reader, is my fervent prayer.

CHAPTER III

My Call To Cuba

Putting Out the Fleece

Being Sure of God's Will in a Matter—Jud. 6:36-40

We have here a beautiful example of God's dealings with His children; and of His willingness to make known in a definite way, His will concerning us. I am doubtful if there are any Christians who do not at times suffer deeply in their desire to know God's full will concerning them, so they can do it. At times we reach crossroads in life's path of duty and it is difficult to know definitely which way we should go, or which of two duties should be taken up as our responsibility. At such times a soul should be still before God, until the path of God's choosing for him is made clear. At one time God laid on Gideon the responsibility of saving the Israelites from the hand of their enemies, the Midianites, and the task seemed so great that Gideon shrank from it. But at last he cried out to God for definite guidance, and he put some fleece out on the floor and prayed that if God was really sending him to do this great work, he would make it clear by letting dew fall heavily upon the fleece and let the earth all around it be dry. If this happened he would then know the divine will. God answered in a clear way. And a few times in my life I have put the "fleece" out to be able to clearly determine the Lord's will.

My call to Cuba was sudden and very unexpected and I felt the step was too great to be taken without definite leadings, It was at the Anderson, Indiana Camp meeting in June, 1930, I closed myself in alone with God one night until 2 p. m. the following day. About 8 a.

m, a burden came on me to put the "fleece" out, and I did so. At that hour, I was practically without money and had been looking to the Lord to supply and I expected Him to do so. Being on the camp-ground, it would have been a very natural thing for some who knew I was going to Cuba as a missionary to give me something; so when I felt burdened to put a financial test out, before the Lord as the "fleece" of direction, in this critical moment, I felt it must be done in such a clear way that there would be no confusion in the matter. So I prayed—asking God to send me some money from some source clear away from the camp-ground, and for it not to be less than $10.00. Anything received on the camp-grounds would not be an answer to this prayer. Much was at stake so I had prayed with all the fervor of my soul, and God sent a definite answer, about 6:30 p. m, I was sitting in the Young People's service when a boy entered with a Special Delivery letter—for me. My hand trembled as I reached for it, because I felt sure it was the "dew falling on the fleece." I was in the presence of God and He was answering. The letter had been sent from Chicago, Illinois, just after mid-day. It read something like this, "My dear Faith, I was burdened for you during the night, and since early morning the weight has hourly grown heavier, and it is on the financial line that I feel burdened. I have scarcely been able to work this morning for thinking of you. I do hope there is nothing wrong. I am rushing this note off to you and hope the enclosed check will be of use to you at this time." Enclosed was $20.00. I had a full answer. The dew had fallen just where I had asked that it might. The gift was *more than ten dollars,* and came from entirely outside the camp, and from one who did not know I was praying about Cuba. Thank God, He has power to remove mountains of difficulties and show Himself strong in behalf of those whose hearts are perfect toward Him.

From the day God sent this clear answer to prayer as an assurance that I was not mistaken in the divine call He had placed on my heart, I moved forward in full preparation for the new field I was to enter. And although nearly twenty-one years have passed, bringing many problems and afflictions and persecutions, yet not once have I doubted my call, and this has brought strength to my soul many times, for knowing as I have that I am here in the center of the Lord's will, I have laid on Him the responsibility of safely bringing me through whatever arises in our work. If our ways are committed to Him, He shall direct our paths. The Psalmist said, "Commit thy way unto the Lord; trust also in Him; and He shall bring it to pass." Praise God forevermore.

God Supplied Fare to Cuba

Knowing definitely that God had called me to Cuba to pour out my life there in getting the true Gospel to the people, I secured the address of one family in Havana, Cuba, and had some correspondence with them. I also had the address of one sister living in Miami, Florida. Having contact with these two places, I made my plans for the trip. I reached Miami, Florida on a Saturday morning, the 6th of September, 1930 and was to leave there by train for Key West at 3:30 a. m. Monday to make connection with the boat from Key West, Florida to Havana, Cuba. I did not come with the backing of the Missionary Board, for although they did heartily sanction my coming, they said they were unable to finance the opening of a new mission field. But believing as I did that I was divinely called to this field, I felt a calm assurance in my heart that God would supply my every need. However, He let me be deeply tested before I got there.

On reaching Miami, I at once made inquiries about the trip expenses, and knowing that on reaching Havana I would need to have a few dollars in hand for a taxi, etc., I found I lacked twenty dollars of having enough so I took the matter to the Lord in earnest prayer. I attended the services in the little church there that morning and evening (on Sunday) and preached in both of the meetings. I passed the day in much prayer—and believed firmly that God would not fail me. Near the close of the night service, a lady came quietly to my side saying she must leave as some neighbor had brought her in from the country and he wanted to go. She slipped an envelope in my hand and quietly went out. I put the envelope in my hand bag, and did not open it until after I was back in Sister Perkin's home, ready to be taken to the train. When at last I opened the envelope and found there the twenty dollars God had sent me in answer to prayer, my heart over-flowed with gratitude to God for this marvelous and clear manifestation of His presence with me. This definite answer to prayer at that time meant more to me than any bank account could have meant. This was to me God's real seal upon my call to Cuba. Praise His Holy name forever. The Sister at whose home I was stopping told me that the Sister who had given this was so poor she could hardly believe it possible that she had made such a gift. After reaching Cuba I wrote to the Sister who gave this offering and told her what it had meant to me. That this had been God's way of getting me to the field He had chosen for me, is an impregnable truth. She then wrote back telling how she had worked and saved this little by little so she could go north to see her aged father who was seriously ill. She told of the struggle she passed through when the Lord told her to bring it all and give it to me. She continued telling how God rewarded her by causing someone who was a stranger to her, and who was going by car to the city where her father lived, to take her all the way without cost, and to also bring her back on their return. Thus a trip that would have cost her double what she had was given her freely for her obedience to the call of God to give what she had in hand. Did not Jesus say, "Give and it shall be given you; good measure, pressed down, shaken together, shall men give into your bosom." Luke 6:38. This experience brings to us very clearly a wonderful lesson. This lesson is that they that put their confidence in the Lord *shall never be put to shame,* for the dear Lord has obligated Himself scripturally to care for them; and we are also taught by this event that God will never fail to reward those who make sacrifice to advance His Kingdom in the hearts of men.

CHAPTER IV

God's "What-So-Ever"—Mk. 11:24

*The outgoing of a passenger boat delayed three days
that prayer might be answered*

A group of God's children were gathered in for a special sunrise prayer service, seeking divine help in the paying of a church indebtedness that was due on this same day. A fervent spirit of prayer rested on many hearts, and we had the assurance that God was going to answer in a marvelous way. After having prayed for some time, Mother Gonzales, a real saint of God, reached over from where she had been praying and quietly called the pastor and me out into a side room and told us that she had the *exact amount* we needed for this church debt in her home and that God had spoken clearly to her, telling her to loan it to us so the bill due could be paid that morning. Then the Lord would send it to us and we could give it back to her. She said it had been sent to pay the passage of three of her little grandchildren to New York, where their parents lived. The parents had asked that they be sent there in company with a lady friend who was sailing the following day. After knowing that the money would need to be on hand that afternoon or early the next morning, to be able to purchase the tickets and properly plan for the trip, we hesitated to accept the use of the money. But the good Sister very definitely declared that God had spoken to her and that she must obey. So we trustingly accepted it and at once paid the bill. That day nothing came to us, and the lady with whom the children were to have been sent grew very angry when she knew what had been done. She declared she was going on that boat (the following day) and that the children would be left behind. But

God, who had given instructions to this dear sister regarding the use of the money, knew full well just how to work it all out. The following day no money came but we felt a great calm in our souls, being assured that the dear Lord would not fail us. In the afternoon, a few hours before time for the passengers to embark, a strong tempest raised, and in the streets trees were up-rooted, small buildings were destroyed, and sailing was impossible. Because of the terrible storm that swept around the coast, the boat was held in the docks for three days overtime. On the morning of the third day, God sent the money in full. The tickets were quickly purchased and the children left on the boat just as they had planned to do. Praise our God! He is the God of the whole universe. He controls the land and seas. He speaks and the waves obey His voice. That evening as the ship went out ploughing its way through the seas, the hearts of a group of God's children in Cuba were singing praises to His name, exalting Him before the people for His mighty power and for His wonderful works to the children of men.

Definitely guided by God's spirit
(Sister Keith's healing)

What wonderful privileges are ours if we are truly living for God, and if we have our lives completely given over to His control. One of the greatest promises Christ ever gave to the believer was that when the Holy Spirit would come that He would guide the children of God into the full light of the Gospel. He said—speaking of the Holy Spirit—"Howbeit, when He, the Spirit of Truth is come, He will guide you into all Truth." This is definitely speaking of the Holy Spirit leading us into the full light and truth of the Scriptures. He will surely do this if we are willing to accept each ray of truth as it is revealed to us by His spirit; but if we reject a part of the Truth, He is not obligated to continue revealing Truth. Our only safety lies in accepting, with grateful hearts, what He does reveal. Then He will continue until our very souls will be illuminated with the light of divine truth. As we follow on in His divine plan, our lives will be filled with grace and victory and glory, and we will then become as lights in the world and draw others to the blessed saviour of men.

There is also another way in which He has promised to guide us, and sad to say, but few of the Christians think of the great privilege that could be theirs; or of their responsibility in magnifying the Lord through these personal demonstrations of His power and of His care. Thank God it is possible for us to hear the voice of God clearly speaking to us, definitely trying to guide us in clear paths of service to Him. In the year, 1929, I had a very definite experience of being guided by the dear Lord in a plain path in service to my fellow man. I lived at that time in Indianapolis and was pastor of one of the congregations. Sister Keith was a faithful member in my congregation. Her general health was good but she had had a few serious heart attacks. These were not very frequent so we had not been deeply concerned about her. She lived a number of blocks from my place, but I usually walked there to see her. One night, possibly 3 o'clock in the morning, I was definitely awakened from sound sleep as if some one had entered the room and called me. As I awakened, I sat up in bed, and after a moment's thought, knowing that I was alone in the apartment, I realized that the Lord had awakened me. So I bowed my head in prayer and asked Him what He had awakened me for. The answer quickly came, "Call a cab at once and go to Sister Keith." I quickly called the cab and rapidly dressed while waiting for it. In a few moments, I was there. Being so definitely sure God had spoken, I expected to see the house lit up, and to see the family stirring for I was sure something was wrong there. To my surprise, everything was in darkness and the family sleeping (as far as I could see). The cab driver stood by a few minutes and the enemy of all good said, "What a foolish thing you have done. They are all in bed asleep." Quickly looking to the Lord I was impressed to enter a small side gate and to try and go around to the back door. I sent the cab away and entered that dark passage for the first time in my life. As I reached the kitchen door, I saw through a small crack, that light was in the house. Without knocking or speaking, I opened the door and entered. There in a chair sat our beloved Sister Keith, to all outward appearances gasping her last breath. She had awakened with heart attack and had gone downstairs for water. When she got downstairs she was so bad she could do nothing. Her husband worked nights and the two daughters were both upstairs in bed asleep. From where she sank down in the chair, with much difficulty she had unlocked the back door. She could not speak a word but as she saw me enter, the tears of gratitude flowed from her eyes. Without a word to her, I stepped to her side and as I laid on hands, I felt invested with authority from Heaven over the affliction. God enabled me to pray the prayer of faith and the work was instantly done. Our praises awoke the girls and they soon joined us. All together, we prayed, worshipped and adored our Saviour and healer. From that hour, Psalms 32:8 has been more real to me than ever before in my life—"I will instruct thee and teach thee in the way in which thou shalt go: I will guide thee with mine eye." "Bless the Lord Oh my soul and all that is within me, bless His Holy Name."

As I write this, I am convinced that some who will read it, will doubt it; but the Lord does not change the fact of truth. Some will say, "But that was twenty years ago. What good does it do us now?" Dear ones, time never has or never will change or take from the power of God. "Jesus Christ the same yesterday, today, and forever—." Some will say, "But that was just one special case." Yes, that was just one special case, but it can be multiplied if we listen to the voice of God's Spirit when He speaks—and then move out in obedience to that voice.

In these latter days, many have fallen from the faith but my brethren, God has not changed. His word of Promise has not changed; neither has His plan for the care of His people changed. What Christ needs today is an army of men and women, spirit filled and humble, ready to sell out, entirely placing their lives in His hand, ready for sacrifice or ready for service. How many will enlist wholeheartedly in His Service—ready to hear, ready to obey, ready to be used by Him to the fullness of your capacity coupled up with the Holy Spirit.

Christ, Our Defence in Times of Storm
Boxes released from the Customs

"He only is our *rock* and our *salvation;* He is my *defence;* I will not be greatly moved." Psalms 62:2.

We have tested, and we have tried Him, and we have proved Him, and we do *know his promises are true;* therefore we shall not be moved by the pressure of exterior things, but shall continue to do as David said, "I will lift up mine eyes unto the hills from whence cometh my help" Psalms 121:1.

In the early part of 1948, kind brethren in the States got together large quantities of clothing, both new and used, and bedding and other household things, and toys and school supplies. They packed seven large packing cases, and shipped them to Havana, Cuba, for us to use for the boys and girls in the Childrens' Homes; and also for distribution among poor workers and other brethren out in the different Mission Stations. How we did rejoice when we got this good news. Rapidly all arrangements were made to meet the requirements for lifting these boxes of useful things from the Customs House. We were informed that the charges would be around $40.00, and we felt this was reasonable, and at the appointed time some of the workers took this money to the Customs House, expecting to bring the things out without further trouble. But we were sadly disappointed as they then informed us that we would have to wait two days more, and pay something over $60.00. We knew this was too much, but feeling there was no way out of it, in sacrifice we got this additional money together. The brethren took it and went back to the Customs House at the appointed time. But our troubles with the Customs officers had begun. At one time they told us that the things were going to cost us over $300.00. We just could not pay this, and kept trying to work on this problem, but the more we worked the more decided these men were against us. At last they told us the things were so dirty and so infected that they could not let them out for any price, but would have to burn them. We still prayed on—trusting God to overrule in some way. Another time they informed us that we could have them out for $700.00. We were so shocked at this news that our hearts almost sank—but we kept saying God's Word just could not be broken, and that He had promised to let us triumph over our enemies.

At this time I had to go to the States to attend some camp meetings, and left Cuba with this great burden still hanging over me. While in the Burnside, Pennsylvania camp meeting, I requested special prayer that God would lay His hand on this thing, and let us have what had been sent for the good of His work in Cuba. How well I do remember that season of prayer. Several took this matter right on their hearts, and when dear Sister J. D. Harmon from Oklahoma prayed, she definitely asked God to take right hold of this thing, and give us those boxes without having to pay anything for them. This seemed like asking almost too much, but does not the Word say to, "ask largely, that our joy may be full." This is what Sister Harmon did, and God answered in just that way. Praise His dear name forever. God worked in a mighty way from that day. Soon after that Brother Horacio Morales, one of our workers in Cuba, was speaking with a man whom he had accidently met, about these boxes and the trouble we were having. The stranger listened attentively, and then said, "You have spoken to the right man—for I am the *defence officer*. He asked for the papers to be taken to him, and at once he took hold of the case. In three weeks he sent word for Brother Morales and I to be ready the next morning, as he was taking us down with him; and that we were going to get the boxes out that day. What a night of rejoicing we did have. The next morning he came early and took us in his car. When we were near the Customs House he stopped at a Military Post and asked that a truck be sent right over to the Customs House with us. His order was obeyed, and we soon arrived there. The gentleman entered the building, taking some policemen with him, and walked in where the boxes were, putting a mark on each one, and asking the policemen to carry them out and put them on the military truck waiting outside. They obeyed and in a few moments we were on our way home, knowing the boxes were also on their way there. God had stepped in and answered prayer, just as it had been presented before Him. The boxes were delivered in good condition, and we did not have to pay even for the truck to bring them out to the Childrens' Home. Praise our God forever and forever.

And the report that the things were in such a bad condition was false, for we never had received a shipment of such splendid things. Brethren, why is it so hard for us to trust the Living God for the things we need, and which He has promised to do for us? May God increase our faith, and help us to so live that He can be honored in "giving us the very desires of our hearts" Psalms 37:4.

As we unpacked and divided out the things for the children in the two Homes and also repacked boxes for the different Mission Stations our hearts overflowed, and we adored and worshipped Our Blessed Lord and Master. Let us love Him more, serve Him better, and trust Him fully for all things.

"ELIJAH'S GOD" STILL LIVES
and
We have the assurance that, "Jesus Christ 'Elijah's
God' is just the same, yesterday, today and forever."
Heb. 13:8

I feel constrained for the glory of God, and for the encouragement of His saints to write a testimony of a very definite answer to prayer which we recently had.

For several years we have suffered a great shortage of water at the Childrens Homes, in Los Pinos, Havana, Cuba. Much of the time the municipality had to send large tanks of water, containing several hundred gallons, and have it poured into our well, to keep the supply going. Last year another well was drilled, but still the same conditions continued. All last winter and spring we had practically no rainfall in Cuba, and a great drought settled down over much of Cuba, and the reports of shortage of water came from all parts of the Island. Here in the city of Havana, where the water supply had never failed, the conditions became so grave that in many parts of the city the water was only turned on a few hours daily, and some days not at all. In Los Pinos where we have the Homes located, we get our water from wells, and these wells all over that suburb went dry. The condition was tragic.

Our well also went dry and we had to hunt from one little farm to another for a few buckets of water. At last folks who had let us have a little water, had to tell us we could get no more as their wells were also going dry. We reported to the City Authorities, and different groups of Government men came out to study the situation and to see what could be done to solve this awful problem for the Institution. A private family could buy water in bottles, and using great care, could get through; but how could we take care of a situation like this in an Institution with over 120 living there? Nothing could be kept clean, no cooking could be done many days, no bathing of the children, no water for laundry work.

One commission came and said we would have to put in a larger electric motor to pump the water. The next group, after much study, said that would do no good, but that the well must be drilled *much* deeper. This sounded more reasonable. But in a few days another commission came to study the situation, and then with sad hearts told us the case was hopeless—that there was *no* water in the earth. They said they had tested it to a great depth, and that there was no sign of water. *That nothing could be done.* The last few weeks before this what little water we had been able to get of a morning was so muddy it could not be used, and at last red clay came up with only a little water in a bucket.

Never have we passed through a deeper problem. No water for cooking, no water for bathing, or cleaning, nothing to drink—a tragic situation and growing graver daily. When the last group of Government men said *nothing could be done,* we turned into the Home almost speechless. We had been praying earnestly, but *we had not yet prayed through*. But at this hour, 2 P. M. on Wednesday, May 10th (1950), a group of the workers of the Homes fell on our faces before God and we cried out of the depth of our hearts for "Water." We forgot everything else, and we prayed for "Water." We had to have water—and at that time God alone could give the water. We did not know *how* it would come as the Government Engineers who had tested the ground had definitely said there was NO water in the earth; but we, like ELIJAH of old, cried out of the depths of our souls for WATER. About 3 P. M. (one hour later) we heard a loud, happy cry ring out over the place. "Water, water, come and see!" "OH, THERE IS WATER—CLEAN, PURE WATER—LOTS OF IT!" We all rushed out to see, and there sure enough, running from all the water pipes, was water—clean—pure water in abundance. Yes, Elijah's God—OUR God—had answered prayer. HE IS THE VERY SAME TODAY.

From that day to this, July 24th, 1951, we have had an abundance of water day and night. In just a few moments neighbors, having heard the cry, came running with buckets to take water to clean or cook. Praise God forever and forever! The Postman heard the news and came hurrying to see if it was true. Others heard of this miracle, and came to see. We had a wonderful opportunity to magnify our God before the people. Thank the dear Lord, the people of this community (mostly Catholics) have had a wonderful opportunity of hearing of the mighty power of God as manifested towards those who love and serve Him.

May God use this testimony for the good of souls. Brethren, we do not trust Him enough, and even when He does answer prayer for us, too many times we fail to give Him the glory. Let us exalt His name together, that the unbelievers may know. And let us live in such vital touch with our Lord that at any time of need, we may just call upon OUR FATHER, and receive the answer full and definite.

"My God shall supply ALL your needs, according to His riches in Glory"
Phil. 4:19

I have already told you of the wonderful way in which God heard and answered prayer in supplying an abundance of water in our dry well on May 10, 1950, and I am happy to tell you that up to this date there has been an abundance of water for every part of the work in the large Institution, and for all the neighbors, since the hour God touched the dry well and sent water. The heavy drought continued for some four months AFTER we had water, and the sufferings around us were terrible, but we had water all this time. Praise God forever!

I have added this note, because many have been writing to me asking if we still have water in that well. Yes, thank God, when He does a thing, He does it well. At the same time we were suffering for water in the Homes, the water condition all over the Island was very grave, and here in Havana, the authorities, in trying to save the water, divided the hours of the day and night in different sections of the city. Out in the Buena Vista Suburb, where we have the mission house, and where the church building is also located (where we always have our Convention), the water was turned on a couple hours late in the night. This made it necessary for someone to remain up in each home, waiting for the water, and then fill vessels to supply water for the family until the following night. Because of these conditions and other problems, the brethren had almost decided that it would not be possible to have our Convention this year. But after much prayer we decided to go on with our plans, and arranged for and bought a number of large vessels for water in the mission house. We always feed the brethren who come to this meeting at the mission house, and it would naturally require much water to carry this through.

I went out to the house with others, two different times to clean and get ready, but could get no water. At last I went out on a Thursday evening to remain with others to catch water in the night for this work. We got the water in our vessels that night, but never needed it. The next morning when we got up we were surprised to find running water. This was just two days before the convention was to begin. We asked our neighbors on all sides if they had running water that morning, and they all said NO. We were the only ones who had, and none of them could understand; but we did, full well. And the water stayed on for just fifteen days—or until all our visitors had gone back to their homes. The day after all had left, the water was again on ONLY in the night for a while so we could get water if we needed it. This condition lasted until October, when the heavy rains broke, and there was more water for the city.

But all during the convention we had a full supply, not only for the cooking and cleaning, but also many of the brethren from out of the city, came to ask the privilege of bathing at our place as they could not get water where they were staying. What a joy to let them come and use of the blessing God had so freely supplied us. How wonderful it is to have a God who really hears and ANSWERS prayer.

But even as I write this I know that some who will read this testimony will doubt it in their hearts. But there are scores of brethren in Cuba who could affirm what I am writing. I am writing this because a number of the dear brethren here have asked me if I had given this testimony, and when I said, "No," they asked me why I did not write it for God's glory. So here it is, clear and straight. The God who withheld rain for Elijah, and later sent rain in answer to his prayer is OUR God, and thank the Lord, He has lost none of His power or willingness. In Tim. 3:5, it speaks of those who have a form of godliness but who deny the power of God. How sad that these conditions exist among those who have all their lives had clear demonstrations of God's love and power, and yet do not believe. Naturally such cannot receive from God these marvelous answers to prayer, *because* He only answers "the prayer of faith," but bless God, those who do really live to the standard of His Holy Word, and whose lives thus please Him, can call upon their Father, and He does answer. May these testimonies strengthen the faith of those who read, and may His great name be lifted up among the people.

A Cow Healed That Money be Supplied for the Mission Work

In the early part of 1950, we were confronted with some unexpected expenses in the work of the Lord. We were praying earnestly for God to move in a special way, supplying the money needed to meet these bills. We prayed several times, but did not feel the assurance we wanted. At last the burden grew on our hearts for the small offerings we were receiving daily would not meet this above the other expenses. When we got right down in earnest we prayed through, and felt the assurance that God had heard, and that according to His promise the answer must come. Had He not said in I John 5:15, "And if we *know* that He hears us, whatsoever we ask of Him, we *know* that we have the petition that we have desired of Him." Bless the Lord, oh, my soul, and all that is within me, bless His Holy Name—He is both able and willing to give us what we need, and ask Him for in Faith.

Believing that our prayers were heard, we arose from our knees and each went our way about the work of the Lord. In four days a letter came from a Northern State, from a stranger. As we opened the letter we had the feeling that this was God's answer. Imagine the thrill as we took out of this letter a check for $200.00. Our hearts overflowed. We called the workers of the HOMES in to rejoice together in another answer to prayer. And our joy was complete as we read the letter. It stated that on a certain day—the day we had prayed through—they had a wonderful experience with the Lord. They were not rich people, but had some cows and depended much on the income from these for the family needs. To their sorrow the best milk cow they had, a good animal, fell very sick, and became paralyzed all over. The veterinary was called but could do nothing for it. So they, in their distress and burden, did the right thing—took it to the Lord in prayer. Went to the Lord for healing for the cow? you ask. Yes, and why not? Has He not said, "If ye abide in me, and my words abide in you (then on these conditions) ask what ye will, and it shall be done unto you."?

These dear ones went in earnest prayer, feeling they must have help, and they told the Lord that if He healed this cow, they would send a good offering for missons. When they went this far—THEN God showed them to send it to Cuba. They prayed, and went to bed. The next morning when the brother went out to attend to the cows, THIS cow was completely well. Praise God forever! So they obeyed Him, and sent the $200.00 offering to us here in Cuba. As we learned of what God had done in order to get the answer to us, we were made to fall down and worship Him who is worthy. The dear ones who sent the offering, did not know us, or the need, but God did and that was sufficient. Oh, that men would learn to believe what the Word of God says, and put their trust in Him for all things. Then could the work of the Lord prosper and many souls would be brought to a definite knowledge of God's great goodness, and His love, and His power. May this testimony encourage some of God's dear children to take all their burdens to the Lord, knowing that He is interested in everything that touches the lives of His children.

God Took a Saint to Glory to Provide Funds for the Convention

In 1950 we were in deep waters economically and were trying the best we could to care for all the different activities of The Missionary Work in Cuba, and at the time of which I am going to speak, we were face to face with the facts that as far as we could see with the natural eye, there were no funds with which to cover the expenses of the Annual Convention, which was to convene from April 23rd over the 30th. Because of the extreme poverty of our brethren, we have always had to pay the fares to and from the convention for the Ministers and workers. We must also furnish food free, not only for these but for nearly all who come, as those who pay their own fare are usually so very poor that this causes the greatest of sacrifice, and they could not come to the Convention at all, if they had to pay for rooms and food. So each year we have very heavy expenses for this meeting, but have always seen such great results that we felt repaid. However, at this time we just knew that unless God stepped in and did something special, we simply could not have the meeting.

A group of workers gathered together to plan and pray and see what we could do. The more we thought of canceling the meeting, the more impossible this seemed, for we are labouring for the salvation of souls, and for the spiritual deepening of God's saints. So after much consideration, we felt we must in some way go through with our usual plans. During this time the spirit of God came upon me in a very special way, as if in prophesy, saying, "God will put this convention through, and supply the needs *if He has to take some saint home to glory to accomplish it.*" As God spoke into my heart, I opened my mouth and repeated it aloud. At once a brother said, "Sister Stewart, what are you doing— prophesying?" I answered saying I did not know about that, but that I was just repeating what God had spoken into my soul. From that hour we went ahead with our plans just as if we had the money in hand. And did we not have it (by faith) since God had spoken out of heaven?

A brother who was present in prayer that day, asked me what I thought it meant for "God to take a saint home to glory to provide for the convention;" and my answer was, "I do not know, but He may know of some poor saint living in a cottage that they will not need, if he takes them home to glory." And that was exactly what God did.

A few days later a dear sister in the Lord wrote to me saying that they had just laid her dear mother, Mrs. Julia Emery, away to rest, as God had taken her. And she continued saying that after returning from the funeral she and her sister had looked through the mothers things together, and had found a letter penned by her, addressed to the two of them, and this is what the letter said, "Dear girls, When you sell Mother's little house, divide the money between the two of you. But please take out first $500.00 and send it to Sister Stewart in Cuba for the work there. Signed, 'Mother.'"

The sister continued in her letter saying that as they read this, they had a feeling that we were urgently in need of the money, so they were not waiting to sell the place before sending this. They had made up what they could and got the rest on a loan, and were sending it at once. The check was sent with this same letter. And needless to say we had the most powerful convention we have ever had in Cuba. God's holy spirit was poured out in every service from the very first until the last—but increasing with each day. Oh, what glory was manifest in those services. And many souls were saved, and sanctified, and several came out of divisions into God's marvelous light, and many sick were healed. Praise God forever. One scripture that just thrills my soul every time I read it is found in Exodus 20:22 "Ye have seen that I have talked with you from heaven." And we certainly know that when God does speak to us from heaven, we are safe in accepting His message, and acting on it. Where faith lays hold of the promises, God cannot fail—for He has pledged Himself to answer the prayer of faith. What the church needs today, in the midst of all the unbelief in the world, is a revival of the old time childlike faith in the Word He hath spoken. Let us as the people of God seek Him for it, as this is what the world today needs to help bring them back to God, and to His ways.

Divine Guidance is Possible Today

How often we have heard folks say they do not want to trouble the Lord about LITTLE THINGS, but He has definitely asked us to bring ALL our burdens to Him. He has promised to be a PRESENT HELP in EVERY TIME OF NEED—so it is our privilege to take EVERYTHING to Him in prayer. And the sooner the true Christian learns this most valuable lesson, the sooner many of his or her problems will be solved, and the pathway (of the just) will then be smoothed out, and the glory of the Lord will shine upon us more and more.

In the summer of 1949, I left Havana, Cuba, arriving in Homestead, Florida on a Thursday evening. I was due to speak in a congregation in Chicago, Illinois on Sunday morning. I had written before to get information about the busses or trains from Miami, Florida to Chicago, and got an answer back from both Homestead and Miami, giving a schedule that leaving Friday morning I could reach Chicago Saturday afternoon. This seemed to me very quick time, but having gotten the same information from two persons, living in different places, I counted on it, and left Havana as before stated, on Thursday. But when I arrived in Homestead I was informed that wrong information had been given from the ticket office, and that the only way I could reach Chicago in time for my appointment would be to 'fly' to Nashville, Tennessee, or to Atlanta, Georgia, and get a bus from there. So I went to the airport early Friday morning, not yet decided to which of these places I would go, but looking to the Lord for direction. It seemed in the natural that it would make NO difference, but God knew what I did not know and He directed my going.

As I stepped to the window to buy my ticket, I placed out *Cuban* money without thinking what I was doing. I was so accustomed to using this. When the agent called my attention to this, I was for the moment confused. As I had been summoned to go on this trip quickly, and in my rushing off, I had failed to change my money into United States currency. (In all my travels this had never happened before.) I was told that to make the exchange there I would lose sixty per cent, and felt I should not do this. Having enough United States money with me to buy the ticket as far as Nashville, Tennessee, I decided to do that. Personally it made no difference to me whether I flew to Nashville or Atlanta. I talked with My Father while buying that ticket, and put the whole thing in His hands. I knew if I had to make the exchange I could do it there in Nashville.

Having good friends in a brother and sister living in Nashville (although I did not expect to have time to see them), after arriving there, I went to the phone to call them. They knew nothing of my plans, did not know that I had left Cuba. On hearing my voice, and knowing who I was, they insisted that I had plenty of time to go out to their home for a few hours and get off on a bus later than I had really planned. So the brother at once drove out to the air field for me, and I was soon happy in their presence.

Remember—God either had to open a way for me to get on to Chicago, or I would have to lose so heavily in making exchange of the Cuban money I had brought with me through my rush in getting off. But almost as soon as I got seated in this sister's home she began telling me how wonderful it seemed that God had brought me there right at that time—for they had been saving their tithe money and had a considerable sum on hand, and at the time I phoned, they had just been talking together about it, and wondering where the Lord would have them send it. At this point in their conversation the phone had rung, and when in surprise the sister—in speaking with me, repeated my name—the husband (who was sitting close by) at once spoke up and said to the wife, "She is coming for our tithe." So the sister hurried into another room and came out, placing in my hand $60.00. What a surprise—and yet why should it have been—for has He not said in His Holy Word that He would direct our paths. In Proverbs 3:6 we read, "Trust in the Lord with all thine heart; and lean not unto thine own understanding. In all thy ways acknowledge Him, and He SHALL DIRECT THY PATHS." And again in Psalms 37:23 we read, "The steps of a good man are directed by the Lord, and He delighteth in his way."

How my very soul thrilled as I looked on that money, knowing that these dear ones knew nothing of this need, and knowing that I could just as well flown to Atlanta, and would have missed all this blessing—but the Lord Himself had directed my ways, and had really prepared these dear ones for for my arrival. With the Psalmist my very soul cries out, "bless the Lord oh, my soul, and forget not all His benefits." May the Lord help us to exalt His name among the people, that others may know of His marvelous works among the children of men—TODAY. Yes, "Jesus Christ (IS) the same—yesterday, TODAY, and forever."

Traveling Expenses Provided Along the Way

In Genesis 18:14, we read where God was speaking to Abraham and said unto him, "Is anything too hard for the Lord?" Again in Jeremiah 32:17, we read the answer to this question, "Ah Lord God! behold, thou has made the heaven and the earth by thy great power and stretched out thy arm, and there is *nothing too hard for thee:*" Praise God forever. If only all of God's dear children could drink in the fullness of this heavenly truth, and profit by it in their lives, what a change would come in the life of many a Christian. Many believe this and say that there is nothing TOO HARD for our God, but they stagger over the little things needed in life, and suffer lack because they feel these things are too small to trouble God with. But it is His delight to come to our aid in the great things of life and in the small things that trouble us.

In the year 1948, I was in the States traveling in the interest of God's work and was visiting a number of camp meetings. In one meeting I was under a heavy burden as I knew I was short of funds, and could not travel without having more. But in this certain meeting no offering was given for missions; neither was anything given to me personally. But on a certain day I had to leave for another meeting in a far-off State, and with a heavy, troubled heart I left where I was, and started for the station. On reaching there I learned that I did not have fare enough to buy a ticket clear through to where I had to go. However, on this long trip I had to make a change at a junction, so bought my ticket just that far—not knowing fully what was ahead of me. Being booked for the next meeting, I felt I must go as far as I could. No one knew I was short of funds but the dear Lord, but that was enough.

I got on the bus, and started, trusting in the Lord to work in some way. I sat down in the only empty seat, but soon found I was seated by a man who had been drinking heavily, and the first part of my trip was very unpleasant as this drunk man molested me constantly. At last a passenger across the aisle got off, and I moved over there. The man who was occupying the seat with me there was refined and kind, and after awhile he learned that I was a returned missionary, and seemed very interested. I gave him a REPORT of our Children's Homes in Cuba, and he settled down to read it, and I dropped off to sleep. After a time I was awakened by him speaking to me, saying he had reached his destination, and was leaving. He put out his hand to me, saying, "Good-bye, and God bless you." He put something in my hand, and at once jumped from the bus, and was out of sight. What a surprise to me, as not one word had been uttered as to how our work was provided for. But when I opened my hand and looked, I had more than what was needed to complete my full trip, even to supplying for good meals along the way. As I left this bus to make my change, instead of having to sit in the station like an orphan, I walked into that station as the daughter of a millionaire (which indeed I am), went into the dining room and had a good meal which I was in need of, and finished my trip, getting to the other camp meeting on scheduled time. Praise the Lord!

I had another experience very similar to this one, in the year of 1950, while traveling in the States. I had finished my work in one camp meeting, and was leaving for the station to go to my next appointment. It was planned for me to leave with a certain brother very early in the morning, and when all was ready another brother minister came to me saying that he had to make a trip at the same time, passing so very close to where I had to get my bus, that he could easily take me there, without the brother who had planned to take me, having to go and thus be absent from the morning service. This change was made, and we started. However, on our way, in talking together of a certain brother's family, the minister who was driving the car said, "Sister Stewart, I believe I can drive past that brother's place for a few moments," which he did. We had a happy but short time of fellowship, but on starting again found that the brother who was driving for me did not have time enough left to get me to my bus, and also for him to get to the radio station where he had to broadcast at that time. He quickly drove to a place asking a brother there to take me, so he could rush to the radio station. This was quickly done, and as this second good brother who took me the last part of the way, drove into the driveway at the station, the bus was there, and I had to enter rapidly. As the brother clasped my hand in saying good-bye, he put a $20 bill in my hand and was gone. What a thrill, what a melting before God, as I knew that this person knew nothing of the condition in which I was starting on that long trip—without funds for trip expenses. It was enough for God to know, and He knowing, had worked out this whole thing, or I would have gone as first planned, and would have had a very difficult time reaching my destination. If we could only get to the place where we would "in all our ways acknowledge Him, He would then direct our paths" and care for us always. Read Proverbs 3:5, 6.

His Answer Never Comes Too Late

Fare provided for tour to some of our new fields

It was in the month of May, 1949. The Annual Convention had just closed and plans were being made to visit some of the far distant fields. Among other places, we planned on making a trip to visit for the first time some new fields that had been added to our work during the recent convention. A good godly minister, who had for years labored alone with God, following the Word as closely as he could understand, not united with any religious group, because he had learned from his deep searching of the Holy Scriptures that God had but one church, and he was praying to be led to this Divine Institution. After long searching and praying God had in a very marvelous way brought him in contact with our work on the Island, through some of our literature. Then he had come to visit us, and later had come to our convention, bringing with him another brother minister, who had been saved under the labors of this good Brother Faustino A. Ramos, and then had later been divinely called of God to the ministry of the Word. These two, after attending the convention, were fully convinced that we had the *truth,* and that the Church of God is the only Biblical church, and they had definitely taken their stand with us, and our work for God. Thus we were planning to visit these brethren in their fields, and to plan together for the work in those parts. But to make the trip a success for God, we needed to plan ahead and inform them when we would be there so that they could properly advertise the meetings. So the date was set, and they made announcements from pulpit, and radio, and through the press. We were to leave here at midday on a Sunday, to reach there in time for a Monday night service.

This trip had been planned at a time when it was necessary for us to pay a number of monthly bills before leaving, and to do this, and have enough for the trip, we needed just $600.00 more than what we had. As the banks here close on Saturday, we would have to have the checks in time to change them on Friday, or we could not get in the bank again until Monday. We prayed and prayed, but the answer did not come. Some brought up questions about the plan—how could it have been of God, and then Friday had passed with no answer yet? But I felt calm in my soul for I have long been dealing with my blessed Lord, and had never known Him to be late with His answers. However, different ones kept reminding me that *this time God had not answered.* Friday passed, and I kept planning and shaping up the work ready to leave. Saturday morning the postman came bringing only one letter, and that was not from one of our regular givers. Were we to be disappointed—what could it all mean? The letter was opened, and a check of exactly $600.00 was drawn out. What praise did fill my soul! What weeping in gratitude! God *had not failed*—no and He never will. Thank the Lord, His promises are safe to stand on.

Even then some could not believe, and reminded me that the banks were all closed, and that I would need to send a telegram to change the dates, and go later. But in a few moments a worker with living faith in the Lord came in and said, "Sister Stewart, give me that check. You sign it, and give it to me, and I will change it." How, where, I did not know, but in faith I signed it, and he went out and in a few moments walked triumphantly into my office, and laid the money down on the desk. Thank God again, and again. "The effectual fervant prayer of a righteous man availeth much." James 5:16. The bills were quickly paid, and everything arranged and the trip made on time, and God's Holy Name was exalted among the people. "Oh that men everywhere would praise the Lord for His wonderful works, and for His goodness to the children of men." After having been in the Ministry of The Word for 58 years, and living exclusively by faith, I can say of a truth "His answers never come too late."

CHAPTER V

The Opening Of The Children's Homes

God Guided with an Unerring Hand

Many times God moves in a mysterious way His wonders to perform. All we need to do is to keep completely sold out to the will of God, willing at all times to let Him have His own way. If there is anything drawing us from the will of God, He can never work out His full plan in our lives; but if our surrender is complete, we need have no fear. He will accomplish all He has designed to accomplish in and through us.

> Surrendered, yes, fully surrendered,
> To Father's most Holy will;
> Where rest, sweet holy rest unbroken
> Sweeps over my soul each day.

Selling out to God brings a soul rest, a peace that cannot be disturbed by exterior things.

In July of 1943, I felt a heavy burden on my heart to open a home for poor children in Havana. During my years of labour in the mission work here, I had suffered keenly at seeing so many homeless little children begging in the streets; sleeping at night on benches in the city parks or in doorways; in the rain and chill of the nights. At last I felt God wanted us to stretch out our hands to help save these helpless little ones. We began praying about it and I felt directed to go to Florida for advice from a few of the ministers before taking such a step. Plans had begun to form in my mind and these I freely laid before the brethren there and met their hearty approval. On leaving Cuba I planned on being back in eight days. That was during the time when we had to travel from one country to another with passports, so as I left the plane in Miami my passport was taken up and I was told to call at the passport department in the Post Office when I was ready to return to Cuba, and get the passport there. A "claim check" was given me for it, so when I was to return, I went to the passport office and presented the claim check. Imagine my surprise when told I had no passport there. I referred to my claim check, and they only calmly replied that they knew it should have been there but that it was not. Nothing could be done about it, but to wait. I waited just *three months* before my lost passport came to light. Knowing my ways had been committed to the Lord, and being assured that "He was abundantly able to keep what I had committed to Him," I decided to calmly wait, and went about doing what I could for souls from day to day. In the meantime, I planned and prayed much about the Children's Home. Having but little money with me, I at last found myself entirely without funds. While in this condition, I received a letter from a Sister in a far off state, saying she had heard I was thinking of opening a home for destitute children, and that she was interested and would like for me to go to see her. Knowing the trip would be an expensive one, and having no money, I decided to write to her thanking her for her letter but explaining the impossibility of making the trip. This same day I visited a dear woman who had lost her husband during the time I was held there in Miami. I spent the afternoon with her and before leaving there, she slipped an envelope into my hand. When I opened it I found I had the price of my passage to the western state to which I had been invited. Two days later God witnessed to my heart that the money was for that purpose, so I went right to the railway station to book up for my trip. I was staying in the home of Brother Oval Cunningham in Miami at that time and as I told them what I was going out for, his reply was, "You will possibly have to book up and wait a month." This would have been true if God had not been planning. But as I stood in line waiting at the ticket window, a passage for Oklahoma City (the city I was booking for) was cancelled and I bought it. This was Saturday night, and I was to take the train leaving Monday morning. When I arrived in Oklahoma City I was given a telegram that had been waiting for me there. It was from Brother Cunningham in Miami telling me that my passport had arrived there the morning I left. God let it be lost to hold me there, so he could work out many things for the future of the Children's Homes. The letter from this sister, inviting me to her home to talk over the plans for the Homes, came in the morning of the same day in which God had moved on a kind heart to supply means for the fare. But he did not let me feel this burden for two days, or I would have booked up, waiting many days for room in the train. He made His will known at the very time when a passage was to be cancelled. Praise our God! Because of having been kept away so long from the work in Cuba, I would have rushed over the very day after getting my passport, had not God so perfectly arranged things that I found myself there in Oklahoma instead. He who was raising up a staunch friend for the Children's work, kept the passport away until I left for the west. How marvelous are His thoughts towards us, and His ways are past finding out. Read Ps. 139:17-18 and Ps. 40:5.

I remained only one day and night with this new found friend and sister, and we freely talked over plans for opening a home for destitute children. I saw this good saint was much touched as she learned of the conditions that existed here, making it necessary for many homeless little ones in Cuba to live in the streets and to beg for food. Although no definite promise of help was made, I left that home feeling assured that my steps had been ordered of the Lord, and that this aged Sister was going to, in some way, fill a place in God's plans for the children's home. When our ways are committed to the Lord, He will lead us in a plain path—that His name may be glorified.

Our First Steps

Soon after returning to Cuba, from the trip just mentioned we opened the children's home in one of our own mission houses—in Santa Fe. From the time our hearts first felt definitely burdened to reach forth a helping hand to the destitute children of this city (Havana) we earnestly prayed as did David of old "Teach me thy way, oh Lord, and lead me in a plain path, because of mine enemies" Psalms 27:11. Feeling how great the undertaking was, and knowing that if we stepped forward even a good work, going ahead of the Lord or without His Divine Leadership, we could not be sure of His provision and His protection, both of which we must have if the work was to succeed. Therefore we steadily looked to Him for guidance. One day I received a check for $10.00 specified clearly "For children's work." This was laid away and in a few days I had $28.00 in the "Special children's fund." This amount of $28.00 is what the work of the Children's Homes was begun with. Some donations of clothing and beds came in and on February 10th, the "Home" was opened and fifteen children were admitted on that day. The most of them were brought from the streets by policemen, and to show God's greatness, I might mention that we had no food supplies on hand for the first meal. In cash, we had only $1.00. No one knew of it but the workers and we just trusted in God—the Father of these little ones. Late in the afternoon a Catholic lady came to the door bringing a dozen hot rolls for the children and on the. tray underneath the rolls lay a dollar bill. A few moments later, another lady called bringing a good supply of oranges and bananas for the little ones. Thus God put His Seal on the Homes and from that day to the present, with now a family of 106 children and 4 workers besides myself, God still supplies our daily needs.

We have sometimes been tested almost to the last hour, but before time for the food to be served, the Lord would move in some way and have it there ready. What a mighty God we do serve and what wonderful things could be accomplished in the work of the Master if only Christian people everywhere would learn to take Him at His Word; and resting on His Divine Promise, move forward in His service giving Him an opportunity of manifesting His compassion and His power in the world. Personally, I am fully convinced that one reason why we do not see more people moved to seek the Lord is that they have not seen enough of the Divine miraculous working power of the Master to be drawn to Him. Did not Jesus say, "And if I be lifted up from the earth, I will draw all men unto me"? Come let us "lift the Saviour up" that the world may see Him as He is in reality.

God Supplied Definitely for Buying the First Home

From our first day in the little home we had opened for destitute children, we saw clearly that God had a larger plan for our activities among the children. We began definitely praying for Him to move on hearts and open the way for us to buy a larger place where we could open the doors to rescue many of Havana's destitute, homeless little ones. The dear Lord began answering prayer in a marvelous way. Although no appeal was made for funds, we soon had $7,000.00 in our Children's Home Building Fund. With this in hand, we began searching for a place, and after some days we found a beautiful place, a site of about seven acres of land, well spotted over with fine fruit trees, and with a large substantial brick house. The place was held at $12,000.00 (twelve thousand dollars). After much prayer, feeling God was definitely directing in the matter, we purchased it. The owner was willing for us to make a down payment of the $7,000.00 we had in hand, and he would then accept the other $5,000.00 in monthly payments; but we let him know that we preferred to do a cash business and that he could expect cash. However, we accepted his kind offer to let us go right away at making alterations. While getting the place ready, we held on to God's promises in a definite way. Has He not said, "If ye abide in me, and my words abide in you, ye shall ask whatsoever ye will, and it shall be done unto you." John 15:7? He knew we had here a little group of saints who were abiding in Him and His Word was abiding in them, so unitedly, we prayed that God would get to us before the time that had been fixed for the transaction of this business, the full amount needed so we could pay cash and be able to meet fully our obligation. God's word declares "Heaven and earth shall pass away, but my word shall not pass away" Matt. 24:35. We therefore believed right through to victory. We were tested to the last day, but on that morning a brother went to the Post Office to get our mail as the postman would leave the office. On his return, he brought the $5,000.00 in full. Praise our God! Oh what a time of melting before the Lord! We had not tongue enough with which to praise Him that afternoon as we transacted the business. We had a wonderful opportunity there, of exalting the name of the Lord before a group of men who knew nothing of the power of God to answer prayer and we did not hesitate to do so. This check came from the sister in Oklahoma whom I had visited while being held in the States because of my passport being lost. "All things work together for good to them that love the Lord, to them who are the called according to His purpose" Rom. 8:28. God had planned my delay in the States to work out one of His great plans in my life and in the work in Cuba. This new Home was dedicated and opened to the public just two months and seven days after we had opened the doors of our little mission in Santa Fe, and had there admitted our first fifteen children. When the work of God is under the full control of a "board of men" no matter how good they may be, the work can go forward only as fast as they can supply funds for it; but when a work is left entirely in the hands of God and moves forward under the direction of the Holy Spirit it has an opportunity to grow and to expand. So as we leaned on the Lord and followed Him, He gently but surely led us forward, accomplishing His own will.

Our Mission Home Building in Havana

Although our new Home was wonderful, it was not long before we realized clearly that although the children's work could at that time be cared for, the general mission work was beginning to suffer. I had lived for some thirteen years in a more central part of the city, and the Mission House (my home) was the center of activities. There, the ministers and workers had freely come with their problems and together we connected and prayed. But as I had to move into the Children's Home to be able to direct it, the ministers and workers were being deprived of this blessing as there was absolutely no place where we could be alone with them. We knew this would greatly affect the mission work in general. A place must be had where the general office work of the mission could be carried on and where workers from over the island could be received and helped.

Again we laid our problem before the Lord, and once more He came to our aid. No public appeals were made for financial help, but the day soon came when we were again brought to our knees in gratitude to Him who never fails to answer the prayer of faith. "If we know that He heareth us, whatsoever we ask, we know that we have the petition that we had desired of Him" I John 5:15. God enabled us to build, right beside the children's home, a good apartment containing the general Missionary Office and living rooms for the missionaries. Praise our God for His loving kindness and His marvelous works. His ways are truly past finding out. The seasons of inspirational fellowship that have been enjoyed in this building have sent their influence out far and wide. The hours spent there in group prayer services have uplifted our work throughout Cuba and other countries. Thank God for our little Missionary Home.

Our Girls' Home

During the first two years in our Children's Home, we had the boys downstairs and the girls upstairs in the building. But as time went on we knew we could not do proper work among them unless we could completely separate the boys from the girls. We were so overcrowded at that time that we were having to turn away some very needy cases. Prayer once more prevailed. We presented before the Father of these orphans, the urgent need of another home. We planned on building but as time went on, we clearly saw the impossibility of this, as the cost of building materials was so extremely high, and many materials were almost impossible to secure even if we had the money. This need grew more and more into a heavy burden on some of our hearts. We cried mightily unto the Lord and He heard us and delivered us. "Call upon me in the day of trouble, and I will deliver you." God is our refuge and strength, a very present help in trouble. Ps. 46:1 Since building was not possible, what could we do? One day early in the morning, I was sitting on the front verandah in meditation and prayer, and this was the outstanding burden of my thoughts. At last I cried out of my very soul, "Oh, my Father, do something for us. Direct our steps in this important matter." Immediately, the answer came through the voice of the spirit of God, "Why don't you buy the lovely home next door?" The home next door—we did not know that home was for sale. How could we have the thought of buying it? But the voice that had spoken was unmistakably that of God's spirit, and He is all wise and makes no mistakes. In a few moments, I sent someone to ask the owner if they were wanting to sell, and the answer was that they would consider an offer. Promptly, three of us went over to look through the house and we were soon convinced that this was all in God's plan. On asking what the price was for the place, the owner replied, "Nothing less than $10,000.00." This was the amount we had in our building fund for the Home. Praise God forever! Before noon of the same day, we had all the papers in the hands of a good lawyer to make sure that everything was clear. Two days later we purchased and paid cash for the place. This added a few more acres to our farm, and this property lay side by side with the grounds of our first Home—both facing to the front on the same public highway—with the mission house and office which had been built the year before, located between the two Homes. None but God could have planned so wonderfully. Trusting God to finish what He had begun, we moved forward planning alterations and also a large addition, and as we worked God worked with us supplying everything needed. On the last day of November 1946, we had a blessed time as large numbers of Christian brethren and friends gathered in to witness the "opening" of the door to our Second Children's Home. As the door swung open, the girls who had long waited for their home, with radiant faces and happy hearts, rushed through the door without any ceremony, taking possession of what God had prepared for them. The boys with no less joy, rushed back to enjoy a freedom in their Home that had been hitherto impossible. From that day we were able to work more effectively than ever before.

The Nursery for Babies

Having several babies brought into the first Children's Home, we separated one room and filled it with only babies. The little ones were cared for in the general Home the best possible, until we had our second home ready to move the girls into. It was then decided to remove the little tots over in the new girls' Home as the older girls were already taking much care of them. However, there were many dangers for the little ones, while living in this home—stair steps, etc., so we began again talking to the dear Lord about the need of a separate Home for infants from a few months of age up to six years of age. The more we considered it and the more we prayed about it, the more we were concerned and convinced that this was also in God's great plan. So we prayed on until prayer again prevailed. How marvelous it is that God never grows weary of our oft' approach to His throne bringing before Him the burdens of our hearts. Praise His Holy Name forever. We selected the building site and prayed on. The day of victory came in mid-summer of the year 1948, and came in a very unexpected way. A nice gift came from dear Mother Emma Meyers, who recently went home to her reward. Mother Meyers had been a faithful minister in the true Church of God for over 50 years. It just seemed to thrill us all as we planned to use her gift for the erection of the nursery building. Although we endeavour to do all our building work as economically as possible, still as the building work went on, it seemed that every workman tried to beautify it as much as possible, as it was to be a shelter for some of God's little lambs. When the building was done, it was lovingly dedicated to our beloved Mother Meyers, and the group of little ones sheltered there will early in life have their little minds filled with pure heavenly thoughts. It would melt your hearts to tears if you could know how some of these babies have been rescued. Could you know the condition of some of their little bodies when they came to us, and then see them as they are today, you would cry out, "What a mighty God we serve."

Little Marcelino was brought to us at the age of one year, and he was nothing but skin and bones. The mother, having tuberculosis, could not give him the breast and she was so poor she could not buy milk for him and he had been fed only with water drained from rice. We took the little bundle in our arms, and breathed a prayer for help. Shortly after this baby was admitted to the Home, three doctors having heard of the case, came to the institution asking permission to examine the baby.

Permission was given, and after they examined it, they frankly told us that its bones were like chalk (and it had no teeth), and that it would never be able even to sit up in bed. They said it would just keep in bed, a helpless bundle. They also said it would be an idiot as its little brain had not developed. I told them we had taken the child in Christ's Name, and that He could make of it what He wanted it to be. About a year and a half later, one of these same doctors was passing the Home and he came in to greet us and see how that body was. I wish you all could have seen the doctor when I called a boy and sent him out to bring in from his sleep, little Marcelino. It was difficult to convince him that this was the same child, not a drop of medicine being given to him. Only good care and much fervent prayer, and today this little boy is one of our healthiest, happiest little ones in the nursery. He is in Kindergarten and learning with the others, and the best of all, he is learning to pray and is being guided gently in the ways of truth and righteousness.

CHAPTER VI

Temporal Needs

"There Hath Not Failed One Word of All His Good Promise"

"There hath not failed one word of all His good promise," I Kings 8:56. We read the marvelous promises of God over and over but as a people we seldom drink in the fullness of these, or stop to apply them to our individual lives as children of God.

We reached a place in our work (in the city of Havana, Cuba) where we definitely had to hear from God. Some bills were due and must be paid on a certain day. Also there was not a penny in hand for transportation in the mission work in the city. Several of the Bible Training School students lived with me in the mission home—and supplies of food were out. We had been diligent in prayer but some way we had not yet reached the throne of God in faith—for does not His Holy Word say, "If we know He heareth us, then we know we have the petition we have desired of Him." Praise God. During the long night hours I was unable to sleep and kept pressing the need before the Lord in fervent prayer. In the early morning hours the blessed Spirit of God spoke definitely in my soul in the words of the text used at the beginning of this testimony. Never did I hear a voice more clearly. God said to my burdened soul "There hath not failed *one word* of *all* His promise." "Bless the Lord oh my soul and all that is within me, bless His Holy Name." I knew the Spirit had spoken through the Holy Scriptures, so I sprang from my bed and searched for this quotation. As I read it, every word was illuminated as with a light from Heaven. When the students arose in the morning and learned of the message I had from Heaven, all hearts were melted and together we worshipped at His feet as we waited for the fulfillment of promise which we knew was on its way. That day an "air mail-special delivery" letter was brought to the door and on opening it we found a gift of one hundred dollars to be used as needed. How our hearts did overflow as we again were strengthened by this wonderful manifestation of His care. The prophet Jeremiah said, speaking of the mercies of the Lord, "They are new every morning." How wonderful! New every morning! Oh! troubled soul, no matter what your needs may be, or what your burden—look away to Jesus. He surrounds us daily with a fresh and bountiful supply of mercies, and He will not fail us, if we confidently trust in Him.

God Is Everywhere

"For the eyes of the Lord run to and fro throughout the whole earth, to shew himself strong in the behalf of them whose heart is perfect toward him. Herein thou hast done foolishly: therefore from henceforth thou shalt have wars." 2 Chronicles 16:9.

What a wonderful thing it is to be a child of God! There are so many marvelous promises given in the Word of God for those who are truly His. If we open our hearts so the Holy Spirit can illuminate our minds and souls, and in this attitude really study these promises, we shall soon find that they actually cover every phase of our lives. Not only the spiritual side, but also the physical and temporal needs. If we are "sold out" to God and definitely "seeking first the things of His Kingdom" His every promise becomes ours; and we have a right to lay hold by faith in prayer, and expect from Him a definite answer in the supply of whatever our need may be.

God's power is so great that when moved by the cry of faith from His children, He reaches forth His mighty hand and does for them, things that are so far beyond the power of any man that we marvel, and are made to cry out from the depths of our soul, "behold the wonderful works of our God." Then we turn our eyes in another direction and we behold His great arms moving to help in the *little things of life*. There is nothing too great and nothing too small for our Father's notice.

It was the week before Christmas in 1948. We were working hard to prepare everything in the Children's Homes in Los Pinos, Havana, for the reception of a number of brethren from the States. But so many things were lacking that it was difficult to arrange. One day the house mother in the girls' home called me to look over several mattresses that just could not serve any longer. As we stood looking at them my heart grew very burdened as I knew we did not have money with which to buy new ones and I also knew there were other things badly needed. In speaking with Sister Claudina, I said, "Sister, we need $100.00 for these things and funds are so low we just cannot buy unless God moves mightily on some heart to supply." We agreed to hold it definitely before the dear Lord in earnest prayer. The following day, one group of our visitors arrived and conditions remained the same. Just as we were serving supper, someone called me to the door and as I stepped out on the verandah, I was greeted by one of our fine young converts who lives some miles out in the country. He, Juan Torre, is the oldest son of a very poor widow. I had not seen him for about one year and was happy indeed to welcome him. He made a very short stay, saying he must return to his work, but that he had come to bring a gift to the Lord. This gift he said, was what he had been able to save in sacrifice during the year and that he felt an urge to bring it and that he wished it to be used for whatever was most needed in the Homes. I could not withhold the praises that were due my Lord Jesus. Right there, I had to honor God and encourage that young saint by telling him how very definitely God had used him to answer prayer. Several inexpensive mattresses and other needed articles were purchased the following day and our hearts not only rejoiced but were strengthened in the faith as once more we beheld the goodness of our Heavenly Father in answering the prayer of faith. Oh that men everywhere could know His love and His power. David in his life had so many experiences of the Divine care that he cried out, "Bless the Lord, oh my soul, and all that is within me bless His Holy Name" Ps. 103:1. At another time, he cried out, *"Let everything that hath breath,* praise the Lord" Ps. 150:6.

Yes, His love is very great towards His children. "The eyes of the Lord run to and fro throughout the whole earth, to shew Himself strong in behalf of those whose heart is perfect toward Him."

Clothing Supplied for Workers in Answer to Prayer

In 1933 we passed some testing times in the mission work in Cuba. Because of economic and political conditions the sufferings among the labouring people were great and these conditions brought many and varied problems in the missionary work. We reached a time when some of our brethren who were either in the active service of the ministry, or who were in the Bible training School definitely preparing for the work, were almost destitute for clothes. Together we prayed and trusted, but the answer was delayed some days. At last a group of workers met and definitely laid this need before the Heavenly Father and just committed it all away to Him.

It was necessary for some of us to make a trip to Santiago de Cuba, a city of some 800 miles from Havana. Four of us started out in the car expecting to drive to a certain place which we would have reached late in the night before stopping; but God planned otherwise. About 5 p. m. we discovered that something was wrong with the car, and we were afraid to continue traveling after night, so we pulled into a garage about 6 p. m. to see what the trouble was. To our disappointment, we learned that the mechanic was not there and would not be until the next morning; so there was nothing for us to do but to go to a hotel and pass the night. The following morning the car was rapidly repaired and we were soon on our way again. Some of the younger ones in our group were inclined to question as to why we had been thus delayed, and had been obliged to pay a hotel bill for the night; but I reminded them of how we had at the beginning of our trip, committed every detail of the journey to the Lord, and that we should be contented with what He permitted to come to pass.

We had not been out on the highway more than a half hour that morning when we saw, right ahead of us, lying in the middle of the highway, a large package. We stopped the car and got out to look at it. For some moments we were afraid to touch it as at that time many bombs were being placed in the highway, as this happened in the days of Revolution in Cuba. However, after spending a few moments in looking at the package, we came to the conclusion that it had dropped off some truck that had passed that way with a load of materials from some factory. The package was placed in the car and care was used to inquire all along the highway at each bus station, if notice had been turned in of a lost package. We advertised in different ways but never had any response. After doing all we could to find the owner and having failed, we opened the box and to our great joy we found we had six new white drill suits (of the best material) right from some factory or store, but we found no mark anywhere that could serve to guide us to the original owner. The suits were of different sizes and fitted the group of minister and workers who had been in such dire need as if they had been made to order. Praise our God forever. The God of the Israelites who made their garments that they waxed not old while they were in the wilderness where they could not get any more, can supply for His trusting children today, "Thy raiment waxed not old upon thee . . . these forty years" Deut. 8:4. Thank God, "He is just the same today" Heb. 13:8.

Had we not had the little trouble with the car we would have passed by that place before the package was dropped. God had planned the whole thing for us. Oh, that we might learn better how to commit our ways unto Him, trust also in Him and let Him bring to pass what should come in each day of our lives. Psalms 37:5.

"A Present Help in Every Time of Need."
Psalms 46:1

In June of 1946 the oldest girl in the Children's Home was very ill, so ill that we had to comply with the laws of the land, in calling a doctor as she was a minor. At this very time, we were without a cent in hand to get even what would be needed for that night for the sick girl. We had been praying and trusting, but it seemed impossible to expect anything, as the mail in the morning had brought nothing, and we do not have a delivery of mail out here in the afternoon. But I stood on the promises of God, and as often as possible I would slip out of the sick room, and into my office alone, pleading with God to move in some miraculous way and supply in this time of great need. Every time I prayed I felt consoled but could see no way for the prayer to be answered, as I thought on it in the natural. The hours wore away, and the child grew worse. Our hearts were sad, but still the assurance kept coming that God, in some way was going to take care of us. Late in the afternoon, one of the workers came to the sick room and called me, saying two gentlemen were in the hall waiting to see me personally. I went in and they came forward introducing themselves, saying that they lived here in the city; but in former years lived in Chicago and had boarded with a certain lady whom I knew. They had recently gone to Chicago on business and naturally had rushed out to see this family where they had formerly boarded. They told how this lady began asking if they knew me, and the work I was doing here in the city for the poor children and when they answered in the negative, she said they must know me, and that to make sure they would really come, she was going to write a letter and send it with them. So here they were to make my acquaintance and to deliver her letter to me. They made a short visit, and as they left, I went into my office to open the

letter—and there was God's answer to our cries. FIFTY DOLLARS, not
sent in a cheque, but in cash, just for ready use. Ho! how wonderful are
God's ways! His mercies are new every morning. The Prophet Jeremiah
said in Lamentations 3:22 "His compassions fail not. They are new every
morning." God not only supplied the temporal needs but the sick child
was soon restored to health. If He feeds the sparrows—cannot He feed
His little children?

"Behold the fowls of the air: for they sow not neither do they reap,
nor gather into barns; yet your heavenly Father feedeth them. Are
ye not much better than they?" Matt. 6:26. Yes, God does care for the
fowls of the air, and we should know in our hearts that He will not let
us suffer unnecessarily if we trust in Him. At the time of which I am
now speaking, I was living in the suburb of Buena Vista, Havana, in
the little mission house. I had four Bible students. They were all girls.
Several young men who were also studying in the Training School, lived
in an apartment close to me. We all lived and worked by faith, trusting
alone in God to supply every need for the work and for us individually.
Thank God, He just never failed us. On a Saturday night after supper,
we were faced with the problem of shortage of food for the following
day. We had what would make breakfast, but NOTHING for the rest of
the day, and our Sundays were our heaviest days of work. We had prayed
and we committed it all away to the Father whose we were. After having
breakfast the following morning, the girls went out to gather children for
Sunday School as was their custom, and then went to Sunday School. I
met them there, and as I entered the building, one of the boy students
came to me saying there was a large package out in the other room with
my name on it. I asked who brought it, and he said a man came and
said a Methodist minister who lived some blocks from there had sent it
by a servant. When Sunday School was over, I asked this same young
brother to kindly carry the package out to the house for me, which he
did. On arriving we opened it, and found everything we needed for good
substantial meals for two days. Yes, everything for the group of workers
and the students. What rejoicing! We knew God Himself had done this
thing, for the gentleman scarcely knew us. I met him only twice, and he
knew nothing of how we lived by faith. At the time of his sending this,
he had no way of knowing anything of our needs but God did know and
that was sufficient. Many times when I think of how God has planned to
take care of us, and of all the wonderful examples He has given us in the
Word, besides all the wonderful promises, I wonder how He must feel

when He sees how little faith the most of the professed Christian people really have in Him. If a good kind earthly father would tell his son, "son, I want you to go to this place and do a certain work for me, and as you know, I am well able and I will supply everything you need, so go on without thinking anything about how you will be looked after, for that is absolutely my responsibility," would a son or daughter have trouble believing the father? Certainly not. But how few are willing and able to take the heavenly Father at His word. Paul has said in Phil. 4:19, "But my God shall supply all my needs, according to His riches in glory." Thank God, Brethren, then let us launch out and prove our trust in Him.

Answer by Cablegram

In the year of 1942, just following our Annual Convention in Havana, Cuba, we had a remarkable experience of answered prayer. Because of the poverty of most of our Christian Brethren, meals were furnished free, but near the end of the convention food supplies were running short and there was no money in hand to meet this need. A very poor sister had her own house rent money in hand and she kindly loaned this to supply the need—naturally expecting that in a few days we would be able to return it to her. But God permitted us to be tested to the utmost that we might have our faith strengthened and that His name which is worthy might be exalted among His people. Day after day passed and nothing came with which I could pay this bill. Two other rent bills for the mission had become due and for the first time in the history of this work we could not meet our obligation. With these three rent bills staring us in the face the spiritual workers cried out of the deep of their souls for God to *intervene* that we might be able to meet our obligations as people of honor. The final test came when we reached the place where if we were not able to meet these bills on *that* day, one mission would have to be closed down, and also the poor widow sister who had kindly loaned the money for the food for the last day of the Convention would be forced to vacate the house where she was living—with no place to go. The night before had been spent in prayer and on this morning a group of us were on our faces before God—*unwaveringly holding the Divine Promises before Our Father who had made them.*

About 8:30 A. M., while we were still in prayer, a telegram was brought to the door. The telegram contained a notice that I was wanted that morning at a certain bank in the city. Our night was turned to day!

Our tears to praises! I hurried down in the city to this bank and there received money that had been sent by cablegram from the States that very morning. I asked for the name and address of the sender and to my great surprise learned that a stranger had sent it. And blessed be the name of Our Lord, the amount was just enough to meet the three rent bills and to furnish the means of transportation that would be needed, with food for the mission workers for the day. "Sufficient unto the day" Matt. 6:34.

From the banker I learned the sender of this precious gift was a perfect stranger to me. I wrote at once to thank them for the gift, and in doing so I told them something of how God had used them to answer prayer in a marvelous way. In replying to my letter they said they had heard of our work for God in Cuba, and had long felt a desire to send a gift, but had been neglectful. They then told how God had laid the burden on their heart more and more until the night before it was sent, they had been unable to sleep as the burden hourly grew heavier, until they promised the Lord they would send it by cablegram as soon as the office opened the next morning. I had never heard of these people and they were in no way connected with the Church of God work, but God knew them and knew where they lived. Thank God. "Call upon me in the day of trouble and *I will deliver thee.*"

God's Care In Little Things

"Therefore take no thought for your life, saying, What shall we eat? or, What shall we drink? or, Where withal shall we be clothed? (For after all these things do the Gentiles seek:) for your heavenly Father knoweth that ye have need of all these things. But seek ye first the Kingdom of God, and His righteousness; and all these things shall be added unto you." Matt. 6:31-33. In this part of Christ's sermon on the mount, we have presented a marvelous picture of His care over His children in the little things of life. We know that our Father has planned that man should earn his daily bread by the sweat of his brow, but He is all wise and He knows that in life's journey many circumstances will arise that we will not in ourselves be able to overcome; and since He is not only all wise but is also all powerful, and all loving, He has kindly taken over on himself the responsibility of meeting all the needs of our daily life, or in other words, our Heavenly Father has planned to help us through all these circumstances that arise in life. In thus planning for our care in every little thing, He has made only one requirement and we must meet that requirement fully, if we expect Him to do His part.

The thing God definitely requires of us is that we "seek first the kingdom of God and His righteousness" and He has promised that if we do, then all these temporal things shall be added. Christ has spoken here in such a sympathetic way—saying, "Your Heavenly Father knoweth that ye have need of all these things—even before ye ask Him" Matt. 6:32. Oh that the dear Lord would help us as His children to grasp the greatness of His love and the beauty and simplicity of His plan for those who truly love and serve Him with sincere hearts. He knoweth just what the human needs are, and He knows just when circumstances develop that throw us into utter dependence on Him, and He has told us to cease worrying and to give ourselves to definitely seeking after the spiritual things with the clear assurance that if we do *seek first spiritual benefits* He will not fail to supply or to work out a way in which our temporal needs will be cared for. Praise God forever for His wonderful plan and for the "exceeding great and precious promises" 2 Peter 1:4.

Beginning with the month of April, 1948, a condition developed which held our mails up, and for several weeks almost no letters reached us. Since our entire work in Cuba is a "work of faith" and most of our offerings come to us through the mails, we were soon in a very difficult position. Day after day, conditions grew more serious. Something had happened, or was happening somewhere that was greatly affecting our income for the work. We took the matter before the Lord in earnest prayer, trusting Him fully, but conditions grew worse. I knew the work all over the island was dependent on us getting prayer through. Other workers and myself were living in the Children's Homes in Los Pinos, Havana, where we had at that time, a family of around ninety including the workers and the children. Our hearts were exceedingly burdened as on investigation, we learned that the mails were tied up in the Post Office because of the political unrest and confusion. It was near time for the Presidential election and we were told that we could not expect a change for the better until after that was over. This increased the burden on our hearts, and as conditions continued to grow more serious the church became united in their burden in prayer. One night while this burden was pressing sore on many hearts, I arose from my bed unable to sleep and sought strength and counsel of the Lord. After refreshing my soul by reading several of the blessed promises, I turned my face to the wall and cried out of the depths of my soul, "Oh Lord speak—I must hear Thy voice. This is Thy work. Help us in some way." Getting up, I again turned to the Word. Without paying any attention to where I was opening the Bible, it fell open to the 20th chapter of Exodus and my eyes became riveted on the 22nd verse, "you have seen that I have spoken with you out of Heaven." Praise God, my burden was gone. He had heard me! Does He not say that if we know that He heareth us, we also know that we do have the petition that we have desired of Him? John 5:15. As I lay there praising God, He reminded me of the parting of the Red Sea and pointed out very clearly that He had done a complete work of deliverance for the people of God at that time. He had not only parted the waters but He had caused the Israelites to pass over on dry ground, and then had sent the waters back to destroy the power of their enemies. Praise the Lord, oh my soul, and all that is within me, bless His Holy name.

I knew victory was coming, for He had spoken out of Heaven. Conditions continued growing worse for two days, but we were anchored on the promises that cannot fail. The second morning after God had so definitely spoken to me, the two Sisters who were cooks in the two Children's Homes both came to tell me that there was absolutely no food of any kind in the house except a few beans (less than half of what we always cooked for one meal). My answer was, "Go and put them on to cook and then go in definite prayer, and I will also be in prayer." All the workers had been in united prayer that morning. In less than an hour, a car drove up in front of the home and a 100-pound sack of the best grade of rice was carried in with other packages. The donor was a Catholic man whom we had only met in a business way. He was at most a stranger to us but God had moved on him to bring food that morning, while we were in prayer for the same. After the gentleman left, I called the cooks and other workers and together we worshipped the Lord in tears of gratitude. And this gift was as the "cloud the size of a man's hand" that Elijah saw when he had prayed long and earnestly for rain. Other gifts came that evening and kept on coming in the days that followed and we could again lift up our heads and say of a truth "behold our God liveth." We serve the very same God that showed Himself strong in behalf of Elijah, Daniel, and others. And thank God we can truthfully say that today "the eyes of the Lord run to and fro throughout the whole earth, to shew Himself strong in behalf of those whose hearts are perfect towards Him." 2 Chronicles 16:9.

CHAPTER VII

Children's Chapter

A Piano In Answer to the Children's Prayers

It is most natural for children reared in true Christian homes to have faith in God, but for the dear little ones in the Children's Homes in Havana it has not been so easy as most of these boys and girls had never heard the name of Jesus except when used in blasphemy, and they knew nothing about answered prayer. After being in the Homes a few months and having attended the Church services where they saw and heard for the first time in their little lives, someone playing the piano, they had a great desire to have an instrument in the Home. They had often talked about their desire and when they understood enough about God, to know that He could and did answer prayer, they began praying for a piano of their own. It seemed they were never tired of reminding Him of this one thing they desired. It was nearing their first Christmas in the Home and as I saw them growing more earnest in their petitions, I asked the Lord to some way take care of this thing in a way that would build up their confidence in Him. Three days before Christmas a letter came for us from a pastor of a congregation in the North and a check for $70.00 was enclosed. The letter ran something like this: "Dear Sister Stewart, a few weeks ago, I announced in our Sunday School that on a certain Sunday we were going to have a love offering to help make a happy Christmas for the boys and girls in the Children's Home in Havana, and I asked that each one bring a small offering. I thought that in this way we would be able to send you a few dollars for sweets for your large family. But imagine my joy and surprise when the offering was counted and we lacked only a few cents of having $70. Someone at once put that in. So here is our gift and remember this is definitely for Christmas for your children."

Many things were needed in the Home, but as I held that gift in my hand, I lifted my heart to God for guidance and I knew that the Lord was making possible the piano. I knelt down and earnestly talked with the Lord about it. The following day, another letter came with $35.00 and this also was a gift for our children's Christmas. This second offering reached us about 9:30 a. m. on the 24th of December. About 11 o'clock the same morning Brother Villafane, our pianist, came hurrying in saying he could not stay long, but that he had come to speak with me about a piano. One of his music pupils, an American lady about to return to the States, was selling out all her belongings. He said she had a good piano, and that he knowing that it was worth much more than the $100.00 she was asking for it, felt he could not hold back and see it go to someone else for he felt we should have music in the Home for the children. I quickly asked how much it would cost to move it out and was told it would cost $5.00. God had sent the full amount, and not a penny more. That evening, the piano was moved into the Home and the children were almost overcome with joy when they really witnessed for the first time in their lives a definite answer to their own prayers.

Praying For Cows

The boys and girls in the orphanage were not having the amount of milk they really needed to build up their little bodies as it was impossible to secure the amount needed out where we lived. Many of them scarcely knew what milk was before coming to us and they could not seem to get enough to satisfy them. We had been trying to get them to the place where they would really listen attentively to the reading of the Scriptures and try to understand what was being read. One evening one of the older girls (in her early teens) was reading the Scripture lesson in the worship period. She had chosen the fiftieth Psalm and was reading the 10th verse when a boy of possibly ten years of age, sprang from his seat and called out, "on how many hills?" I at once caught the inspiration of the child and asked Rafaela to slowly read the last verse over. She read again "for every beast of the forest is mine, and *the cattle on a thousand* hills" (this is verse 10). As he caught the words, his eyes grew wide with wonder and his innermost thoughts came out, "Oh, oh, and can't He give us some?"

Another caught the thought and turned to me with a pointed question. "Grandmother! (this is what the children in the Home call me) if we are good children and we pray will God not give us some of those cows?" (Oh, for the simple faith of a child.) I could only answer, "I believe He will."

They began praying with all the earnestness of their souls and they did not grow weary at praying as older folks often do, but they kept right at it. At last their childish faith conquered. A letter came from a Christian brother in a far-off State, bringing a good offering and saying that he was thinking about the children in the Homes and wondered if we had our own cows. He continued saying that if we did have, then we could use the offering for whatever else was needed, but if we did not have, then we should buy two cows. We called the children in and had a thanksgiving service, praising God for answering the children's prayers again, and then sent two men out into the country to buy the cows. Two good cows were bought, one with a calf. These reached their new home one morning during school hours, and were first brought through the front gate of the institution. As the cows called out their first greeting to the children, every eye was turned in the direction from whence it came, and as soon as the boys saw the lovely animals, they forgot all about lessons and to the amazement of the teacher, they jumped over desks and took a short cut out to where the cows were waiting. School was dismissed for the day as that was the greatest day the children had ever known and we did not want to quench their happy spirit. Later in the day, when the fever of their joy had worn off, we called them all together and again read the precious Psalm (that many of them call the "cow Psalm"). Then together we worshipped the Lord and praised Him for answered prayer.

Praying for Meat . . . When God Speaks, the Answer Must Come.

During the first world war, I was engaged in missionary work in far off dark India. Although I was active in general mission work my principal responsibility was in connection with orphanage work. A girls' home was first opened and some years later a similar home was founded for boys. During my first years there, although I was then connected with the Church of God missionary board whose headquarters are in Anderson, Indiana; and although they did at times send a little help for the work, yet during the first nine years of my labours in that field, our work was carried on by faith as the board assumed no responsibility in the financing of the work I was doing. They only sent in a brotherly way, what they could from time to time. Our experiences were so great and the many answers to prayer so marvelous, that I could write volumes and not tell it all. During those years we frequently had to say as did the Psalmist of old, "The Lord hath done great things for us, whereof I am glad." However, I am not going to use much time or space telling of what great things He did for us twenty or thirty years ago but since He is "just the same today," I shall confine the testimonies of this book mainly to the manifestations of God's power in recent years. In this chapter for children, I am going to use an incident that happened in the work there, especially where His love and His care for His "little lambs" was so clearly manifested.

At one time, during the war, it was very difficult to get meat, and at one time the girls in the Home got very hungry for meat. Knowing as they did that those years of war brought on us what we did not have before, they said nothing to me or the other workers about their great desire to have meat, but a group of the older ones (then from 10 to 14 years of age) got together and went far out from the house under the shade trees and there they had a good prayer meeting, laying their desires right out before their heavenly Father in full confidence that he would grant their petition. Later, in telling me all about it, they said they at first had asked the Lord to send either money or meat, but after considering it awhile, one of them said to the other, "but girls if God sends money, Mama will not know it is for meat when there are so many needs, and she will surely buy something else with it." So they went in prayer again and asked the Lord not to send money, but to please send meat. I knew nothing about this simple, childish prayer, but I did know that for two days the girls kept right up around the house. Many times during these days I urged them to go out under the shade where it was cooler, but to no avail. About noon of the second day (after they had prayed) a man came to the home with a large basket of meat on his head. A note was brought from the sender telling me that the meat was for the children in the Home. The girls were even then on the back verandah listening to what the man was saying and by the time I got the meat back to them, they were simply overcome with the great joy that filled their young hearts as they realized their prayer was fully answered. I rejoiced with them, and we mingled our tears of gratitude together and adored our Saviour and Friend, as they related to me their experience of taking their desire before the Lord and then waiting for the promised answer.

The following day, I called on Mrs. White, the lady who had been used of God to help answer the children's prayer. As I related to her how earnestly they had prayed, and how they had waited the two days in full assurance of faith, she wept bitter tears and said, "Miss Stewart, I am so ashamed of myself," and she continued saying that they (her family) had two sheep, and cared much for them, and that just two days before she had sent the meat, God had spoken clearly to her, telling her to have a certain one of these sheep butchered and to send the meat over to the Girls' Home. She told how she had refused to do so, and that on the following morning when she went out to open the door of the little house where the sheep were kept, she found the very one God had called for, dead on the floor. At once, she was convinced that God had taken the animal because she had withheld it, and refused to obey Him. So at once, she and her husband called a butcher asking him to kill and dress the meat of the other sheep so that it could be sent to the Children's Home.

Thus God again, proved His faithfulness in answering prayer; although it had only been children who had their desires before the Lord. Has He not promised that "the *desire* of the righteous shall be granted?" Yes, thank God, and even children can love and serve the Lord and can get their prayers through and have them answered. And if prayer is sometimes delayed in its answer, never cast away your confidence, for "though it tarry, wait for it, for it shall surely come." Hab. 2:3.

God Answers Prayer—And Stays the Rain

It was a Saturday morning, and everything in the Children's Home in India was in commotion. It had been definitely planned to take lunch and go to the riverside that afternoon, letting the children have a good time out in the open air. They were so happy about it all. But it was understood the work must all be done up nicely before going—so they were doing their very best. Everyone who was large enough was putting their strength right into the work, and planning on a wonderful time that afternoon.

No sooner was dinner over, than the clouds began to gather and the sky darkened. Then the rain began to fall. What a disappointment it was to all. But these dear children had before this learned that God was their Father, and also that He definitely answers prayer—for those who trust in Him. It was not many moments until the children themselves had a conference, and then away they went, some to one bedroom and some to another. They began praying, but every few moments some child would slip out on the verandah to look up at the sky to see if it was clearing. And sure enough, the rain suddenly stopped, and then although the sky was still dark, the faith of these children could not be daunted. God, their Father, had answered their prayers and stopped the rain, and could they not trust Him to finish what He had begun? They insisted that it would not rain and began getting ready. So we honored their faith, and started. However, at that time we had a sister missionary from another part of India visiting in the Home, and she took her umbrella with her. The children remonstrated, but her faith was not equal to the test. The children, knowing they had asked "in faith" for God to clear the day so they could go, and He had stopped the rain, they were certain He would not then disappoint them. Why should anyone take with them something to protect them against the rain—just as if they did not expect a full answer. (This is the way the most of God's grown up children do.)

The riverside was soon reached and oh, what a joyful time they all had! They played and sang and had their lunch and near night they all returned to the Home. Not a drop of rain had fallen during all that time, giving them a happy afternoon in answer to prayer. But just as they entered the Home the rain began pouring down and it rained all that night. This was even more convincing to the children that God had in His plan an afternoon of rain, but He held it back in answer to their childish prayer of faith.

What a lesson to these dear little ones. They could never forget it, and it was deeply engraved on the tables of their hearts that God loves to answer prayer. This should be a lesson to the Lord's BIG children also, and we should all take Him at His Word, rest on His promises, and honor Him by asking largely that our joy may be full, and also that His dear name may be lifted up among the people.

God Can Answer Prayer or He Can Withhold

During my years in Mission Work in India we had some marvelous experiences in God's dealings with us in the children's work, and I am writing this experience for the benefit of little children everywhere. God is not only the God of the older folks, but He is just as truly FATHER GOD to all the little children who love Him and trust Him. But it is absolutely necessary for children (as well as older ones) to keep their little hearts and lives clean if they want God to answer their prayers.

What I am going to write about now contains TWO precious lessons for all the dear boys and girls who shall read this chapter. My prayer for you is that God will bless and help each one to understand both these lessons, and your lives will be richer and fuller if you do.

In the Girls' Home in India the children soon learned that God was their Father, and that He loves them and would answer their prayers. They usually loved to pray and ask Him for the things they needed—and they just expected to get them in answer to their prayers, for He had answered them so many times.

One day a group of them came to me asking if I thought God would send them a lot of candy if they were to ask Him—for they said they really were hungry for some good candy. This was during the first world war, and things were very hard with us, and naturally we could not afford to buy this for so many children. They feared that since it was something they did not really need, He might not answer their prayers. God reminded me of the verse that says, "Delight thyself also in the Lord; and He shall give thee the desires of thine heart." Psalms 37:4. I reminded them of this verse and had them memorize it, for their own use. At last their faith was lifted up, and they went in prayer for the candy. They prayed earnestly and believed, and in a few days they were not at all surprised when a big car drove in front of the Home, and a gentleman came in saying that his young daughters were just home from boarding school, and that they had been making some good candies, and had brought them over for the children. We did not know this family before—but God did know them, and had used them to answer the prayer of the children. And what a large amount they had brought! Oh, what a happy time they did have and how they did enjoy those sweets. First, naturally, because they were so delicious. But that was not all. These children had learned to love the Lord so much, and knowing He had heard their prayers and had sent them, made them so happy while they were eating them. They really did thank the Lord for this lovely gift.

But after all this beautiful lesson in faith was learned, they had a very hard experience as the devil tried to spoil it all for them. At the time the wonderful treat of sweets was brought to the Home, two of the teachers were away and their sweets were put on a plate, and placed on the table in the workers dining room. When the teachers returned, they were told about the visitors, and what they had brought, and that their portion was kept in the dining room for them, they were so thankful and hurriedly went to get the sweets. But to our amazement, there were NO sweets for them. The plate was there—but it was empty. What a surprise! Knowing that no one else had entered the home, we rang the bell and called the children all together and tried to find out who was guilty of stealing someone else's candy. No one confessed—all said they knew nothing about it. A gloom and sadness settled down over the Home, for TRUTH had been held at a high standard there. Days passed, and at last with the heavy work that always belonged to the Institution, and other things that naturally came with each passing day, many forgot this incident of "the stolen sweets," but a few of us could not forget it, and prayed earnestly that a lifetime lesson would be brought to the children in some way. Covered sin grieves God, and too, He has said "to be sure your sin will find you out," and this is true. Sin just cannot be long covered.

One day we found the food supplies were very short, and by the evening meal there was only about half enough, and although we prayed, God did not send any more. This condition continued for four days, each day just enough food coming for the smallest children to have their full supply, but for the others a very skimp supply, until they were really hungry. This had never happened before in the Home. We prayed, but we knew something was hindering.

The climax came on a Sunday afternoon. We knew the children were hungry, and oh, how we suffered in realizing this, but our great burden was for God to clear the spiritual sky in the Home, as we knew prayer had not gone through. That evening after the smaller ones were tucked in bed, all the others gathered in the living room, and as I sat there in a low chair, most of the girls were sitting on the floor, Indian fashion. I talked heart to heart to them, and told them we knew God was withholding and that there must be a real heart searching to find out who was guilty. As I talked on, one dear girl about 10 years old, broke up in the deep of her little heart, and arose and said, "Oh, pray for me—I am the guilty one. I stole those sweets long ago, and hid them and ate them. No one else had anything to do with it. I have suffered so much seeing you all suffer, and now I must confess my sin. Do forgive me, and pray for me." What a breaking up we did have, and how God did bless in that season of prayer. As we finished, and this dear girl gave a clear testimony of God's pardon, we all went to bed, satisfied that God would now answer. Early the next morning the postman brought the mail, and one letter had a good supply of money. Oh, praise God, He does not fail! But imagine our surprise when we saw by the postmarks, that the letter had been in that Post Office just four days. God had kept it hidden, or in some way kept it from coming through—until the sin was out of the way. Then He quickly got it on its way, and supplied all the needs.

My dear children who are reading this—remember always that God cannot bless when you try to cover sin. Always be open hearted and sincere, and then when you have a need you can, with pure hearts call on God for help, and He will answer. From that day, we frequently heard the children speak of this incident, and of how necessary it, was for them always to do the right if they wanted God to help them in time of need. So God taught us two very precious lessons through this experience.

CHAPTER VIII

Divine Healing

"The Prayer of Faith Shall Save the Sick"
James 5:15

The Remarkable Story of E. Faith Stewart's Serious Illness and Healing

Some of we brethren who were eye witnesses of Sister Stewart's serious illness and her remarkable healing in the spring of 1945 feel constrained by the spirit of God to write some of the facts concerning this healing as an inspiration to the faith of those who shall read it. However, let us say that it will be quite impossible for anyone who did not see her during her illness to really comprehend just what God did do for her. And our only desire in writing this is that God's name may be glorified and that poor, discouraged, suffering ones, reading this may be encouraged to put their trust in the One Who Never Fails.

On December 29th, 1944, Sister Stewart, in closing a three day ministers' meeting (in Havana, Cuba) preached the most powerful sermon on divine healing that we had ever heard her preach in the fourteen years she had been here in missionary work (up to that date). In her message she urged the brethren to lay hold and maintain at any cost the blessed doctrines of the Church of the Living God. She spoke strongly of how the doctrines of the Bible had been lowered in the church in many places, but that we here in Cuba must see to it that every Bible doctrine be definitely TAUGHT and PRACTICED. She said that we as God's people here MUST hold the standard even at the very greatest cost. And that many times God had to let sufferings come to the faithful ones that His Word be preserved, as the Lord had to have instruments through which he could work, and Sister Stewart continued saying that if God ever wanted her as an instrument through which to work out His glory, she wanted to be submissive and true.

She continued saying, "My brethren, if I ever get so sick that I am unconscious, where I cannot fight 'the good fight of faith' myself, I urge you for Jesus sake and for the sake of my reputation as one who for many years has definitely trusted alone in God as my healer, to just leave me entirely in His hands. If I ever get to where you feel that medical help is the only thing that would save my life, then just let me die, going into His presence just as I have lived. For I would choose death in His will, rather than to extend life in any other way.".

The day after having put this solemn charge on the church, she left for Punto San Juan, Camaguey, a distance of some 400 miles from Havana, to hold a two day assembly meeting with a few congregations in that district. She returned from there on January 3rd, and two days later was taken very ill. As we saw from the first that her illness was serious, a doctor was called just to examine her (to comply with the law). He said her condition was very grave indeed. He said her's was a case of gallstones, and that to save her life an immediate operation would be necessary—but he also said that her heart condition was so serious that it would not permit operating. What a sad condition she would have been in if her trust had been in the uncertain arm of flesh. How thankful we all were that we knew her trust was alone in God, and that He was able.

A few days later Sister Stewart was removed to Buena Vista (another section of the city of Havana), where she would be closer to the congregation and could have better care. Soon complications set in and it required a group of faithful ones to divide their time, and care for her night and day. Two days after removing her, she lost all consciousness and also had a 'stroke' which made her entirely helpless. The church building was close by, and the doors were never closed day or night during her entire illness, for groups of brothers and sisters were constantly there holding on to God in earnest united prayer for God to spare her life. Cablegrams were sent to many in the States and they replied that many there were also holding on for victory.

As we watched our beloved sister sinking lower and lower, another doctor was called in to examine her, so if she passed away there would be no trouble with the law. The first doctor who had examined her had turned so bitter because she was not sent to the hospital for the operation (although he could give no hopes), that we felt it unsafe to not call another. This one said her case was hopeless and that he could not understand how she was living, and said it then could be only a matter of a few more hours. Hundreds of brethren and friends from all over this part of the Island came in to see our sister, and looked on her with sad hearts.

At last one night, about 10 o'clock, the toot of an ambulance was heard, and in walked a doctor and nurse with a friend of ours. This gentleman friend said to some of the brethren that he had personally paid for a private room in the hospital and had come to take Miss Stewart there to see what could be done. He said, "Miss Stewart is dying and something must be done at once." Several of the brethren answered and told them that before losing consciousness Miss Stewart had herself put on them the solemn responsibility of leaving her definitely in God's hands alone, if she got unconscious where she could not stand for her own desire, and they felt they could not submit to her being taken, knowing as they did that it was against her desires. Then the doctor told us that if she was not allowed to be taken, and if she died, (as she would) some of the brethren would be handled by law for manslaughter. They also told us that the Federation of Doctors would take a hand in this. We pointed out to the doctor that all over the land, men are dying for the sake of principles which many times do not amount to anything—then what would it matter if some of us did have to suffer a little for standing for a principle of Divine Truth, founded on God's Word.

We do thank the brethren here and in the North who stood solidly during this long, severe test. The church in Cuba had never experienced anything like this before, but God gave sufficient grace. The first doctor who examined Sister Stewart, said this case was a case of slow murder, and that when she died (for of course they knew she would die) he would see to it that not one of the several doctors who had examined her should give a certificate for burial. But thank God, while these were waiting for the hour when they could plunge God's people here into confusion (as they thought) and great trouble, God was working out His own great plan for the glory of His name.

Our sister lay in this condition—entirely unconscious for 29 days. But the PRAYER OF FAITH PREVAILED. On a Friday night God gave the witness that prayer had gone through, and although slight signs of improvement were visible, still God let us be tested, and she remained unconscious until the following Sunday morning when to the great joy of those watching her, her eyes opened. This was the morning of February 9th, and as different ones rushed to her side and spoke, she recognized each one by their voice, although her vision had not yet returned. The first one who reached her side and spoke to her, was the friend who had formerly brought the ambulance and doctor, to take her away by force, to the hospital.

Sister Stewart had to learn to eat again, and had to learn to walk, etc. She was as one having been completely gone from this world, being restored. Praise our God forever. Glory be to His matchless name! Her strength began to return and one month later she was able to go in a car to the city to attend to some business. She had gone down in flesh from a weight of 168 pounds, to around 90 pounds. The day she went into the city, just one month after her healing, she was weighed, and had gained until that day she weighed just 100 pounds. What a mighty God we do serve! Oh that men everywhere would learn to trust in God for all things. Truly the mouths of the gainsayers were stopped, and our Christ was exhalted among the people. And as Sister Stewart once more walked the streets of this city, going in and out among the people in her ministry of service to humanity, many were blessed and were made to believe in Our Living God as never before. Truly *they that trust in the Lord shall never be confounded or put to shame.* Bless the Lord, oh, my soul and all that is within me, bless His Holy Name.

Signed:

MR. JOSE CAMPINS, Pastor,
Church of God, Almendares, Havana, Cuba

MRS. M. CAMPINS, Assistant Pastor,
Church of God, Almendares, Havana, Cuba

ERASMO TEXIDOR, Evangelist

MRS. AMERICA SUAREZ, Pastor,
Church of God, St. Fe, Cuba

This is one testimony of healing that I could not personally write, as much as I might want to, for I was so completely dead to everything, that I only know what the brethren tell me. As far as I know, no one who saw me during this illness has ever seen anyone else in the condition I was in, living on to tell the story. Never shall I forget the burden that gripped at my heart the 29th of December, 1944, when I preached in the last service of our three day ministers' and workers' meeting. Having watched the drift that had been coming in on the church in the States, and having suffered deeply over seeing the blessed standard of God's Holy Word let down, my soul was stirred and I did heavy preaching in that three day meeting, and my special burden was that we as The Church of God in Cuba, definitely take our stand (and keep it), to keep the full unadulterated Word of Eternal Truth right up in the place God, Himself, has put it, and not allow compromise of any kind to enter our work. My last message was on Divine Healing of the body, and that message of Truth burns in my very soul yet today. God's Word is unchanging; His promises are DIVINE (not human); therefore, they cannot be *broken* or *changed.*

Although I had not said much about my physical condition, I knew well that unless God worked a miracle in my body I could not long be with the little church in Cuba, and my soul was heavily moved. Would they be able to stand in the persecutions that I believed were soon coming on us, and to keep up the standard of *Truth* where God wanted it kept, or would they weaken. Would their courage and faith hold out? So out of a burdened heart I spoke, and thank God the message of Truth had a definite response from the hearts of many of our number. Thank God for brethren who could stand such a test, and say with David, "Though we walk through the valley of the shadow of death, we shall fear no evil, for thou are with us, and thy rod and thy staff, they comfort me." At the time I took my bed I weighed 168 pounds, and when I got up, or when God touched my body in healing, I weighed around 90 pounds. After being well nourished for exactly one month (after getting out of bed) I made my first trip out in a car, and went to the bank. That day I just balanced 100 pounds. Thank God, He soon brought me back to normal, and I have now put in more than six years of the hardest work I ever put through. Never have I at any time in past life carried the amount of heavy responsibility and put through such excessive work as in these past six years. Praise God from whom all blessings flow, He is still the very same Christ of God, and none of His promised have lost any of their power. If you want a fulfillment of His promises in your life, be sure to *live to the full standard,* and to *teach* the *full* standard, and keep your life entirely hidden away in His will, and the promises are yours. Here in Cuba we are still going right on with the good old time TRUTH and it is good enough for us. We are not seeking any easier or broader way. Praise God forever! Yours in defense of the FULL GOSPEL.

Healing of Blind Eyes

Truly we are living in a day of infidelity and unbelief; and as children of God we need to seek every means possible to keep our faith in God and in His unfailing promises alive. If the devil can destroy faith in the great power of God, it will not be long until the entire plan of redemption will become vague, and the very foundation of everything spiritual will go right out from under us, and our religion will then be only a dead form, even denying the power of God, and we shall be carried into the whirlpool of sure destruction. My brethren, awake, and renew your search of the Holy Scriptures, and pray through until the fire of the Holy Spirit will be kindled anew in your hearts (if you have lost it) and His promises will become real to you, and you will be able to have the daily benefits of His power working in your behalf.

I personally know scores of men and women today, who at one time trusted God for their healing just as definitely as I do today, but who slipped somewhere along "life's highway," and today they not only do not trust their own bodies in God's powerful hand, but they ridicule those who really do get answers from the Lord. But if I believe the Bible to be God's inspired Word of Truth, then I must believe the promises He has given us, and must act like I believe it. The world of sinners around us will never know anything of God's divine power, and of our privilege of living where the blessings promised may be ours, UNLESS we as Christians have a living demonstration of the fulfillment of these "promises" in our own lives. Let us let the Word of God be demonstrated through us, so unbelievers will be converted and drawn to our Christ.

In the year of 1923, while laboring in India as a missionary, I began to suffer much with my eyes. At first, I thought it was because I was at that time staying in Puri, where there was but little grass or green foliage to rest the yes; but the great stretches of white sand, with the glaring sun casting its rays on this, and I thought that when I would return to Cuttack, India, I would be relieved of this trouble. But it was not so. I went back to the Childrens' Home where I had lived many years, but my eyes kept getting worse. The constant burning of the eye balls was almost more than I could endure, and too, I could no longer see with the glasses I had. I then went to Calcutta to have glasses fitted. This was carefully done by one of the best opticians, and I returned to Cuttack to await the day when I would receive the new glasses, expecting them to be a great help. It was possibly ten days before the glasses came, and great was my disappointment when I found I could not see with them. Believing some mistake had been made, I was taken again to Calcutta to the same optician, and he carefully listened and then examined my eyes again, and told us there had been a great change in my sight from the day I had been there before. Again he carefully tested the eyes, and I returned again to Cuttack to await the glasses, but this time with some doubts as to the results. When the glasses came, and I tried them on I could only weep, for I could not use them. There was nothing to do but to return to the city, and tell the doctor of my great disappointment. All this time the suffering was increasing, and at times I felt I could not endure it longer. This time the optician said he would not make any attempt at fitting glasses to my eyes, until I would go to a specialist to whom he was sending me, and that if after examination he said I could be fitted, he would try his best. I was taken to this specialist, and was soon told that I would never wear glasses again. We all knew what that meant—and went back home with sad hearts. The day after reaching the Home in Cuttack I spent much time in secret prayer, deepening my consecration, and making my decision to be true in trusting God to the end, no matter what that might mean. He sent comfort to my soul, and I settled down to await His time. I had been suffering then about seven months, and at this time was almost blind. I could only faintly see objects, and daily the sight was dimmer. In about three weeks more I was blind, and remained this way nearly *seven* months. God only knows the suffering, and the sadness. But He did comfort, and help me to get adjusted to my lot, and I went on with as much as possible of my work. All the time I was meditating on the Great Promises of His Word, and feeding my soul on these, my faith was growing. Thank God for the Power of His Word. At last a time was set for prayer and fasting by the great Church of God at large. But even before the date set for special prayer—God by His Spirit laid the burden for my healing on many hearts and we began to get letters telling of this burden. Six days before the date that had been fixed for special fasting and prayer, a letter came bringing an anointed handkerchief. This had been prepared by some ministers who definitely believed then in the power of God to answer prayer. When other missionaries in the HOME saw this, they rejoiced and read the letter to me, telling of how God had laid the burden so definitely on their hearts to have united prayer, and anoint the handkerchief, and send it to me, as the apostle Paul had done while in his ministry, (and others) and had seen the mighty results in the healing of the afflicted. As the letter was read we all felt that was God's day to heal, and our faith was definitely lifted up. Some faithful Indian brethren were called in for united prayer at 4 P. M. that day, and the anointed handkerchief was applied to my eyes. The power of God touched me and I saw "as through a mist darkly" but rapidly the mist cleared away and by bed time I could see the stars of the heavens above. Praise God forever and forever. The next morning I took my Bible and sat down to weep and read from His Holy Word, the first time I had been able to do this in almost a year. Some five months had elapsed while I was losing my sight, and I then passed almost seven full months BLIND. I want to emphasize the fact that *I was blind, and NOW I see!* Glory be to His matchless name. I put emphasis on this, as it has been reported, and used as a weapon against God's holy cause, *that I was not blind.* God's Word tells us of a class of people who will even deny the very power of God, and still profess to be His, and the Word warns us just what to do to save our own souls. Let us read carefully from 2 Tim. 3:4-5, "Traitors, heady, high-minded, lovers of pleasure more than lovers of God, Having a form of godliness, but *denying* the power thereof; FROM SUCH TURN AWAY." Praise God this is what I had to do, and now His blessings still fill my soul, and thrill my being as I live in the place where PRAYER IS STILL ANSWERED for those whose hearts are perfect towards Him.

For the benefit of those who read, I am inserting here a letter which I received from the optician who had worked so hard to fit me with glasses, and failed because my sight was fast going. The healing of my eyes took place April 1, 1924.

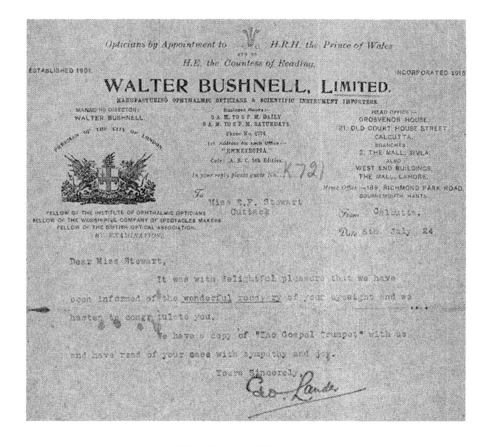

FAITH STEWART HEALED
Anderson, Ind., April 3, 1924

A cablegram just received here announces the healing of Faith Stewart. No particulars are given. This information is being sent to inspire you and your congregation in the healing services of April 6.

J. W. Phelps.

A mailing card, reprinted above from an original copy, was mailed from Anderson, Indiana, prior to the April 6 meeting.

Healed of Heart Dropsy

In the winter and spring of 1936, I was in very poor health and found it almost impossible to carry on my mission work. I suffered greatly from shortness of breath and fatigue. My feet became more and more swollen, they were so bad that sometimes as I walked the streets people would turn and look back at me, and I have had brethren and sisters remonstrate against me trying to go out at all. I never did stop my activities in the Lord's work as long as I could keep going at all. My teacher in Spanish during my early days in Cuba happened to be a medical student, and by the time of which I am now speaking he was a practicing physician. When the time came that I felt my case was serious, I went to this medical friend to consult with him that I might know how to care for myself and what I could safely eat to nourish my body, but with no idea of accepting any medical aid and I frankly told him so. He examined me and was shocked at seeing me in the condition that I was in. He sent me home to go to bed and stay there, and told me he would come out the following morning to see me. How well I remember that visit. He told me that if I had a family here, I would never know what he was then going to tell me. Since I was absolutely alone in Cuba, he would have to come out frankly and tell me my true condition so I could personally do my best to help myself. Knowing me as he did, he knew it would be useless to even suggest medicine but he made out a diet, forbidding the use of any salt or lard or meats. In fact, in a few days, all foods but milk and juices were taken from me. I was propped up straight in the bed and forbidden to lay down at all, as the physician said I was in the last stages of *Heart dropsy* and that even if I had wanted medicine, very little if anything could have been done for me. When the doctor gave his verdict, I was alone in the house with a small child who was staying with me. After he had gone, I had the child close my door and go out. There, alone with my Bible and my God,. I fought the battle out. In tears, I asked the Lord to direct my reading and without knowing where the Bible would open I let it fall open to the 20th chapter of 2nd Kings and I began reading. As I read the first verse where the Lord sent the prophet to tell Hezekiah *"thus saith the Lord, set thine house in order, for thou shalt die and not live,"* I wept before God and searched my heart until the very presence of the Lord literally filled the room with His Glory. Then I said, "Oh, Lord, I thank thee that all is well with my soul. I have nothing to fix up." An hour like that is when hearts are truly sincere for they know they are very definitely in the presence of the Lord God. Glory filled my being and alone there I wept in joy. Later, I continued reading of how Hezekiah wept before the Lord and of how God sent the prophet again to tell him his prayer had been heard and that fifteen years would be added to his life (read from 2 Kings 20:1-6). Thank God yet today, God's true servants can pray through and by the power of prayer can change things. This is what we might call effective praying. Prayer that does something! Prayer that brings forth fruits! God still hears the heart cry of His children; He still sees the tears of confidence that flow from those who in afflictions press right through trusting Him to the very end. That morning God assured me He would heal me. But the battle was long and hard. Eleven weeks passed with me daily growing worse. All this time I was forced to sit upright against pillows. My legs became so heavy that I, of my little strength, could not move them to change my position. My body was rapidly filling up with poison and daily, my condition grew worse. How well I remember the day when the doctor friend (former teacher) told me very definitely that my days were numbered and that there was not one ray of hope for me physically. On getting this information, all my personal belongings were divided out and I was waiting to go (if that was His will). But during these long months my comfort by day and my pillow by night was John 15:7, "If ye abide in me and my words abide in you (then in this condition) ask what ye will, and it shall be done unto you." This promise is as broad as the entire span of life, and so deep that it reaches away down far below the deepest suffering we ever could have. "Bless the Lord, oh my soul, and all that is within me, bless His Holy Name"—forever. At last from the poison that was filling my body, dark spots came out all over me. This doctor friend had to leave me on Sunday night for the States and before leaving, he made out my death certificate and called another doctor and showed it to him telling him that he would be notified when it was all over, and for him to kindly fill in the date and the hour. This happened on Sunday afternoon; I lived on but on Tuesday following, my feet touched the chilly waters as I was going down in the valley of the shadow of death. When I could no longer speak to man, I still had communion with the Lord and I kept quoting John 15:7. "If ye abide in me, and my words abide in you, ask whatsoever ye will, and it shall be given." I would say in my heart "Lord, *all* I ask is *extended life for Cuba.*" At last all I could do was to say, "Lord Jesus—John 15:7," and at last I could only say in my soul, "Lord, Cuba."

This was on Tuesday evening. That night a call was sent to Brother Calloway, at that time, pastor of the Church of God in Jacksonville, Florida. He was urged to come by the first plane as I was dying and they wanted a minister from the States. By 9 A. M. Wednesday, he was at my bedside and quietly prayed. At the close of his prayer, I said in a whisper "death is rebuked." I lingered in the same condition over two days and one night. Death was rebuked but there was no visible change. That second night the congregation met at the church to pray for me all night. Prayer prevailed. I was *definitely* healed. Through the early morning hours, I slept as I had not done for three months. The weary watchers by my bed seeing the change went out to rest a little and from over-fatigue, they slept soundly. On getting up and finding me lying right on my left side, they thought I was dead but thank God I was healed—healed by divine power. Two days later I was taken for a long drive and ten days later when Brother Calloway left for the States, he left me in the pulpit in the Church in Buena Vista, Havana, preaching to the congregation.

Dear ones, would you like to have an experience as glorious as this one? You may have some day, but remember that to have this you would have to travel the same road of suffering and go all the way that the Lord marks out. Christ never could have passed through the glories of the Ressurection morning if he had not first gone through Gethsemane, and to Calvary.

The standard of healing has been so lowered through the terrible apostacy that has swept in among those who profess to be truly His, that it is not easy to obtain real healing for one does not even know (in many places) *who to call* to obey the Word (Jas. 5:14) and pray the prayer of faith. Even among those who at one time trusted God for their own bodies, can be found many who will refuse to believe this testimony, but praise God forever, there are scores of people living right around us today who know it is true.

CHAPTER IX

Testimony Of Others

The Day of Divine Healing Is Not Past

I want to give a clear testimony of how God heard prayer and healed me in 1935. For many years, I had suffered terribly with asthma, and it seemed I got worse as the years went by. Many times I called for prayer, and God would give definite relief but later another attack would come to me. Every year all during the cold season I would have repeated attacks and such very hard ones that at times it seemed I could not endure it longer. Then in mercy God would again answer prayer and give help, but I lived in fear of the next attack. Anyone who has never suffered with this disease, knows nothing of the agony and sore distress. This condition had gone on for years but thank God at last a day came when my faith was actually lifted up and the work was definitely done, the disease was gone, never to return.

At last while in a very severe attack we called the brethren and they came out to our home and obeyed the word of God (James 5:14-15). As they prayed, my faith took hold in a definite way and prayer went through. The work was done. Thank God from that very hour, I have had no return of this disease. All who knew me then, know now of a truth that the Lord healed me. Brethren, His word is true, and let us trust Him at all times. He will give the answer.

Another Case of Healing in Our Family

In the year 1944, we moved from Havana to the other end of the island to open the work of the Lord there. Shortly after moving my family to that place (Guantanamo), Oriente, one of our boys took very ill with fever. Each day he grew worse. Naturally, we were praying because for many years we have definitely trusted God alone as our healer, and he seemed to have a change for the better. As I was then working for an American construction company some little distance away from home, thinking the boy would be all right, I returned to my work. On my return home at the end of the week, to see the family and attend to the services on Sunday, my wife told me that the boy had been bad all the week with a very high fever. That Sunday morning a friend came to the house and began talking hard to me, saying something had to be done as the chills from which the boy was suffering had worsened. He had been burning up with fever for eight days. My friend left at mid-night and many other friends came and tried to force us to do something. Later, one of these friends sent a woman there (a spiritualist) to anoint the child. My daughter met her at the door and on learning what she had come for, told her we did not believe in anything connected with spiritualism, and could not allow her to enter the house. Our friends did not even ask what we wanted but sent whom they chose. While these people were around trying to insist on us doing something, we were quietly but firmly trusting that God would intervene.

I called my wife and told her I was sending a telegram to Havana to Brother Barnes, asking the Brethren to get hold of God with us, for Lloyd's healing. On Monday morning I left and returned to my work with a burdened heart. I went to the overseer's office and told him my son was very ill and I wanted a leave of absence. It was granted and I returned at once to the bedside of the child. I took my place at his side, and told my wife I was not going to let many people in. I was just staying right there to hold onto God. Tuesday he was in the same condition but we continued trusting in the Lord. Our faith was strengthened by a telegram from Havana saying the Church was praying with us, and for us to hold right on. Wednesday morning still brought no change. My wife and I were determined to take God at His word and stay right there. Thursday the touch came and his body cooled, and Friday he sat up and on Sunday, three days after God touched him, he was up to stay; healed by God's divine power. He has never had a touch of the disease from that day to this. Thank God, it pays to hold still with fervent prayer, while the test lasts and hold right on for victory. Jesus healed in Galilee, and He is just the same today. I could write a book on the experiences we have had of God healing in our family and healing others too, by prayers we offered for them. Read Heb. 11:6 and 2 Kings 20:8.

Yours in the One Body in Christ,

Signed: THOMAS S. FRENCH,
Guantanamo, Oriente, Cuba

Marvelous Healing of Tuberculosis of the Spine
(See Pictures Page 116-117)

Dear Sister Stewart,

I am so glad to write to tell you of little Frankie's healing. I really thought someone had done so long ago. In the autumn of 1944, Frankie was sitting on the arm of a porch glider. He fell off backwards and struck his little back across the edge of the cement porch. However, we did not think he was seriously injured until about six weeks later when a lump formed on his spinal column. Soon he began to have great difficulty in walking. We then became alarmed and took him to a baby specialist who ordered him to be X-rayed. The X-rays revealed tuberculosis of the spine, and the doctor said it was caused from that fall. They placed him on a board frame, lying on his back, so he would have to lie there quietly so the T. B. germ could not work. For two long years he showed no improvement at all, then he seemed a little better and in December of 1947, they operated on his spine. In this operation the doctors took pieces of bone from the shin bone and placed them on his spine bone, to strengthen it so it would not bend. But after the operation, he was worse. Then in the spring of 1948 they said he would be down on his back on that frame for two years more at least, and that it was possible little Frankie would never walk again. I thought I simply could not take two more years of it, although Frankie had been quite cheerful all the time.

I was later asked to bring Frankie to the Church of God, as you were going to be there, and that you would pray for him. As you know I did take him and you prayed for him, and right after that he wanted to get up, and said he was healed, but we followed the doctor's advice and kept him on the board frame. But we saw a great change in him from the very time he was prayed for. He began to move more, his appetite increased and his general health was so much improved. You prayed for him in June and the next time he was X-rayed which was in September following, the doctors ordered him up off the frame, after having said plainly that it would be at least two years before he could get up. They saw the remarkable change in his spine and it was easy to see what God had done, just by looking at the X-rays. This is very marvelous in our eyes, and we are praising God for putting Frankie on his feet again, so he could play with other children. He was on that frame just four years and four months. That was surely one test. But today our boy runs and plays just like other children and is enjoying life, all through God's goodness to him and to us. If we only believe, God will never fail us. Pray for us that we may always do God's will and be faithful.

In deep gratitude,

Signed: Mrs. Berniece Watson,
Kirkland, Indiana

Dear Sister Stewart,

Enclosed you will find a testimony of little Frankie Watson's wonderful healing as written by his Mother, who is now SISTER WATSON. The reason I say she is NOW Sister Watson is because at the time of Frankie's healing neither she nor Frankie's stepfather were Christians. But thank God, now through the influence of this wonderful healing, they are both converted and on fire for God.

I would like to make some additions to Sister Watson's letter. The night that we all agreed in prayer for the healing of Frankie, after prayer he wanted to get right up off the canvas board and stand up, but due to the fears of the Mother who was then still a sinner, she would not let him. But on the following Saturday (it was on Thursday night that you prayed the prayer of faith for the child) he was taken to the hospital for an examination and X-rays, but the doctor would not examine him as it was three months before the appointed time for them to give him an examination. When asked why they wanted him examined so soon, Mrs. Watson told them frankly that she thought Frankie was healed because he had been prayed for. The doctor then told her that this was rank foolishness and he definitely would not examine him then.

As Sister Watson has said—Frankie was kept on that board and in a plaster paris cast for another three months, all the time wanting to get up and walk as he believed God had healed him. But this privilege was denied him until he was taken to the hospital again at the appointed time. X-rays were then taken and to their surprise they found NO signs of any defect in little Frankie's spine. Praise God his spine was perfect! This was to the surprise of the doctor because at the time of the last examination before this, he had told them that it would be *at least* two years before Frankie would be up, and that it was possible he would NEVER walk again. This was just six months after the doctor had made that statement. After the X-ray pictures were developed and brought in the doctor looked at them with surprise, and then he would look at the child and then at the mother. He could not figure out what had happened. But thanks be to God, we know what had happened. God had marvelously healed Frankie's spine. He is now running and playing just as other children do, and is becoming stronger every day. What a mighty God we do serve.

I am enclosing a picture of Frankie taken while he was in the cast and laying on the board, and another one taken as he is now.

Signed Matt and Edna Cook, Pastors,
Church of God, Kirkland, Indiana

A Definite Healing of Appendicitis

On February 16, 1948, God marvelously healed Earl Davis, son of Mr. and Mrs. John Davis, of Farmland, Indiana, of a serious case of appendicitis. Earl, then 13 years old, was very sick all night on a Sunday, and on Monday morning the parents took him to Muncie to be examined. Three doctors examined him and were definitely agreed in their decision. They all said to get him to the hospital AT ONCE, as he had a very serious case of appendicitis and that they would operate on him at five p. m. that same day.

The father was away working at the time, but was called and came at once, and they hurried the boy to the hospital. But while there waiting for him to be admitted they called me by telephone and asked me what I thought they should do in an emergency like that. (At this time I was their pastor.) I told them that he was their child, and naturally they were the ones who would have to decide what to do; but that I knew full well just what I would do under similar circumstances. I would definitely trust God. But they were the ones who must make the decision for this child. The father told me that after having talked with the boy himself, and knowing how Earl felt, he just felt he could not force him to go through the operation. I then told them that if they decided definitely to leave the boy in the Lord's hands, to bring him out to our house and we would have prayer for him there. So in a short time here they came, bringing Earl out for prayer, having left the hospital.

He was very pale, and was suffering intensely. We anointed him with oil, as God's Word tells us to do, and prayed for his complete healing, and God gave the healing touch instantly and did a mighty work in his body. However, according to the father's own words, others in the family were not satisfied with this, and just could not believe it was really done. So the next day they took Earl to another doctor in Farmland, and had him give a thorough examination, just as the other three doctors had done the day before. But this doctor said to the parents after the examination, "Friends, I cannot find any symptoms of appendicitis." And then they told

FRANKIE WATSON HEALED OF
TUBERCULOSIS OF THE SPINE

after four years and four months strapped to a board frame.

The pictures below show Frankie as he was strapped to the board frame, and then after his complete healing.

(See story on page 112)

him about the decision of the three other doctors. At hearing this the doctor said, "Well, this puts me on the spot—so bring him back tomorrow at 2 P. M. and I'll give him another check up." This was done, and at the end the doctor said, "I still say I cannot find any symptoms of appendicitis, and he may go back to school tomorrow." Thursday night Earl was out at prayer meeting, and again the next Sunday, and he has been perfectly well ever since. There is nothing too hard for OUR GOD.

Another Healing in the Same Congregation

Sister Mary Coun, one of the members of the Smithfield congregation, was so sleepy after eating her dinner on July 7, 1948, that she lay down and slept so soundly and so long that her daughter who lived with her became alarmed and tried to awaken her, but found it almost impossible. All that night the daughter watched her, trying at different times to awaken her, but could scarcely arouse her at all. The next morning they called a doctor to learn what her trouble was. On examination the doctor told the daughter that the mother had the "Sleeping" disease and that nothing could be done for her.

Sister Coun had trusted the Lord for her healing for many long years. She was a faithful child of God and that night we stopped at her home on our way to the prayer meeting, as she and her mother usually came over with us. As we stopped in front of their home, the daughter came running out to us, weeping, telling of the sad condition of her mother. She was much wrought up, because they had lived together so long, and meant so much to each other. I was late and we had to hurry on, but we promised to return after the service was over. This we did, and Brother and Sister George Lykins, Sister Bertha Smith and others went with us. In the service that night we had definite prayer for the sister, and the daughter told us that she aroused some for a time. Then we again had earnest prayer, asking God for her complete healing. The dear Lord answered prayer, and when I went to see her the next day she was much better, and on Sunday, July 11th, she sat out on the porch with friends and even walked around in the yard. That week end she was back in the Church services with us; healed by the mighty power of our God. Again our hearts were made to rejoice in His great love and in His wonderful care.

Signed: MRS. ELIZABETH VANNATER

Saved and Healed

I desire to give my testimony as to how I first was brought in touch with the blessed Gospel of Christ, and oh, how He worked in my heart! I consider it a privilege and an honour to do this. I was born of Catholic parents and carefully reared in a good home, but I knew nothing of the Gospel until less than four years ago. I trust that this testimony of my experience with the Lord may serve as a blessing to some who, like myself, did not have the privilege of knowing Him as their Saviour early in life.

I had known of Sister E. Faith Stewart, and of the Children's Home she had at the time some distance from my home, but never had any personal contact with her or Christianity until in 1944 when the terrific cyclone passed over this end of Cuba. I first entered the Home during those hours of terrible suffering and danger, with a group of Red Cross men as we were out doing what lay in our power to help relieve suffering humanity at that time. Seeing a large group of helpless children in the condition they were plunged into through the cyclone, I could do no less than serve them to the best of my ability. But little did I know what that touch with Christian people was going to mean to me in the future. My visits to this Institution did not end with the ending of the problems created by the cyclone, but I continued to visit there frequently, as something had made a deep impression one way or the other on me. I found myself with a deep realization of the lack of something that I saw in the workers at the Home. I often wondered if I ever could be like they are. The spiritual work I saw being accomplished there interested me as the days passed, and the shining faces of the workers were an inspiration. The daily life of these Christians and their treatment of all who went there, was distinct from what I had been accustomed to seeing. I did not then understand that the thing that made them so different was the experience they had of Christ reigning in their hearts. Today I see it clearly, because He is reigning definitely in my heart also. During my first several months of contact with the Gospel, I went day after day to the Home just to watch, and as I saw them happily serving the Lord and the people, I longed to know Christ myself. Sister Stewart was constantly talking with me of God's love and His power, and of His plan for our salvation. She gave me tracts to read and these gave me more light and truth. The more I read and heard of God's plan, the better I understood what caused the vacaricy in my heart. I lacked Christ in my heart and life. When it came time for the annual Convention, the following April, I attended and there I surrendered my heart to God and definitely sought His pardoning grace. Since that night I have never lacked His divine help or direction.

For some time before my contact with the Gospel I was losing my sight, and I got to where I suffered constantly and many days could scarcely see to do anything. It seemed that I, a young man of 26 years, was going to be sightless, or nearly so, and that life would not mean much to me. After being saved, the brethren in the Church of God began praying for my eyes, and God healed them com, pletelv, Now, I have no difficulty in carrying on my work and my studies. Praise the Lord.

God has also definitely spoken to my heart, call, ing me to study to prepare for the work of the min. istry, that I may be a soul winner for Him. He has definitely called me to be a "fisher-of-men." His grace is burning in my soul and I want to bring men and women out of darkness and deception, since I have been brought out into the glorious light of the Gospel. With God's help, I am doing what I can to help in the work among the children in the Homes and also out in some of the missions of the city here. At the same time, I am studying in the Bible Training School of the Church of God in Havana, Cuba, preparing to give my whole life to God's service. Since my conversion I have suffer, ed some very deep persecutions and trials, but every moment the dear Lord has been with me, walking right by my side. The Home for poor children where I was first brought by accident, to do my part in giving relief in a time of great danger, is where I now am living, co-operating with the workers here while studying and preparing for my future life's work. We are labouring here, not only to care for these children, but to help build real character, and we are trying above all to bring them to Christ, so some day we may have the joy of seeing them go out into the world, noble hearted Christian men and women. From morning until night I am daily giving thanks to God for having ever searched me out, and having revealed the Gospel Light to me, and saving my soul and for sanctifying me definitely by a second definite work of grace. For having called me to His blessed service, I want to give the good message of salvation to the lost and search out souls and bring liberty to the captive souls. Isaiah 61.

May God use this testimony of my experiences as an inspiration to many young people who have talents, to consecrate them to the Lord and prepare them to be workers for Him in fields where the "harvest is truly great, but the labourers are so few." Pray for me that I be eternally true to my God.

Signed: HORACIa MORALES.

The Touch of His Hand Makes Whole

"Behold, happy is the man whom God correcteth; Therefore despise not thou the chastening of the Almighty: For He maketh sore and bindeth up: He woundeth, and His hands make whole." Job 5:17-18.

Praise God for His tender love and His marvelous works to the children of men, and especially to those who love and serve Him and who put their whole trust in Him, and in His precious Promises.

As I begin writing these testimonies for God's glory and for the encouragement of my suffering brethren, I feel very unworthy of all He has done for me and for my family. I can truly say His promises are true and we can depend on them. As I meditate on His goodness the words of the Psalmist flood my soul, "Because He hath set his love upon me, therefore I will deliver him: I will set him on high because he hath known my name. He shall call upon me and I will answer him: I will be with him in trouble; I will deliver him, and honour him. With long life will I satisfy him, and shew him my salvation." Psalms 91:14-16.

Our first little daughter, Dorcas, was bom almost without life. For some time before her birth the doctors gave but little hope, and after her birth NO hope of her living. But long before she opened her eyes in this world, wife and I placed this little one entirely in the hands of the Lord for all time. And in the sad days and nights that followed her arrival in our humble home, as we watched her little form almost fading away God gave us comfort. Besides other afflictions she had a very serious case of asthma from birth. She had no desire for nourishment and could retain but little of what she did take. This condition, coupled together with a nervous sleeplessness made her little life hard indeed. She lived on, but was only skin and bones. Many times it seemed she would surely leave us. But we knew many of our faithful brethren were holding on to God with us in prayer and as often as we fell to our knees pleading for help, He did give it. Praise His holy name forever. But still He permitted us to be tested. At last we had little Dorcas examined just to see if there was anything lacking in the care we were giving her, and when she was examined the doctors told us plainly that there was nothing that could be done to help her; that no one could reach her case. However, this did not trouble us as we had no idea of putting her in the doctor's care. Our full trust was in the God who had given her life.

Being a minister of the gospel, I had definitely been preaching the Bible standard of divine healing and had prayed the prayer of faith for the healing of many sick ones. And although we were tested severely, persistent faith triumphed at last, and the gentle but powerful hand of God at last touched little Dorcas and healed her completely. Appetite was given her, she slept well, had no more attacks of asthma, and in a short time was a happy, healthy child. To God be all the glory.

The enemy of our souls was not satisfied with the sufferings he had brought on us through the long and serious affliction of our little daughter, but in 1946 he laid the hand of affliction heavily upon my own body. I had for years preached the healing of our own bodies as a part of our atonement heritage and had gone in and out among the people praying for the sick, and now I was down under the heavy hand of affliction myself. I had a very bad case of hemorrhoids and the suffering at times was almost unbearable. In only a few weeks I lost over ten pounds in weight, and from the excessive loss of blood I became so weak I could not continue with my work. I cried out to God from the deep of my soul, and many times I had instant relief through my own prayers and those of my brethren, but the affliction continued to grow worse. At one time while I was at the very worst, some brethren feeling my sufferings so much advised me to go in for an operation, and pointed out the fact that this would not be a serious operation, and that I would very soon be well and at work again. The devil stood right there with his temptation, but God, by His Holy Spirit lifted up the standard of faith against the enemy and helped me to keep my eyes steadily on the dear Lord. The day came when God saw I had been tempted and tested enough for that time, and He laid His powerful hand on my afflicted body and did a complete work of healing. And my faith and that of many others was strengthened and His dear name was truly glorified. Dear brother and sister, put your confidence in the Lord Jesus and be steadfast and unmovable in your trust and He will never disappoint your soul.

In my work in the ministry among the people, I have seen the mighty hand of God extended to heal cancerous ulcers; to heal a leper girl; and have seen the healing of a young man who had been paralyzed from his childhood. Thank the Lord! "God's hand is not shortened that it cannot save; neither his ear heavy that He cannot hear; but your iniquities have separated between you and your God, and your sins have hid His face from you, so that He will not hear." What a clear message of instruction we have here in Isa. 56:1-2. Again Paul said, "Jesus Christ the same yesterday, today and forever." Heb. 13:8. Praise His name forever. Suffering one, examine your own life in the Light of His Word, and if you find you are living a life that is pleasing to Him, then resist the devil and all unbelief, with all your soul and firmly put your case in His hands and He WILL answer prayer and heal you. May these testimonies be a blessing to many a suffering one, is my prayer.

Yours in the FAITH that was once delivered to the saints,

Signed: ERASMO TEXIDOR
Santiago de Cuba

Death Rebuked and Child Healed

This testimony of Divine Healing is given for the glory of God and for the encouragement of other afflicted ones. It is also given to let the world know that even in these dark days of apostasy when we are surrounded by so much unbelief, we, The Living Church of God, STILL believe in God's power to hear, or to answer prayer giving us any help we may have need of, if we only live for His glory and really trust Him. Yes, we still believe that when we obey the clear instructions given in His Word in James 5:14-16, the answer will come.

At the time of the incident of which I am writing I was engaged in ministerial and missionary work in Punto San Juan, Camaguey, Cuba. Close to the Church of God mission where I lived was a Catholic family who had several small children. I began visiting them, and after some time, had the joy of seeing the children who were old enough, regular attendants of the Church of God Sunday School. After these children had attended for some time, one night the parents sent me word that one of the little ones was very sick; yes, seriously ill. I immediately went over to their house and found the child indeed in a very critical condition. The Mother sat holding it, and the child looked even then as if the stamp of death was on it. The case was so grave that five doctors had gathered in a council over the case, and medical science had entered in a solid battle to try to save the little life. They were fighting the disease with all the power they had at their command.

The Mother of the child was also afflicted, so seeing the condition I took my place definitely in this critical hour, and never left them during the entire struggle. As a missionary, or servant of the Lord, it was my duty to serve them, and "to weep with those who wept." And while serving, I kept quietly praying, and even fasting, and quietly dropping a word about God's love and His power whenever I had an opportunity. Although everything was done that medical science could do the child grew rapidly worse. Its eyes became fixed, and did not move. The tongue also became immovable, and the whole little body laid as one dead. FIFTEEN days passed in this crisis, the parents living through many hours of agony, not knowing when the end would come. At last, at the end of this fifteen days, the doctor in attendance called me to one side and said they (the doctors) had gone to the limit of the power of medical science, and that there was nothing more they could do. He said that he took his hands, and was leaving the child in my hands. Turning away, he said, "Possibly your God can save this life. We can do no more." This was a solemn moment for me—this doctor and the family and nearly everyone around us were Catholics. As the doctor went sadly away—I humbled my heart before God and humbly thanked the Lord for the decision of the doctor. I knew this was the moment when God could have an opportunity of proving His divine power and His compassion. Since the doctor had said plainly that medical science could do no more, but that possibly OUR GOD could save the life, I had in my heart a plain clear conviction that God would heal the child and get glory to His own name. I knew it would require a miracle as the child was more dead than alive then—but man's extremity IS God's opportunity of demonstrating His power before the unbelieving world.

After the doctor had talked with me and left, I went to the parents and told them all he had said; and asked them what they wanted to do— if they definitely wanted to put the child in God's hands, and trust Him. Their answer was prompt and definite. They said, "Yes, we do." I then quietly gathered up the injections and all other medicines they had, and threw them into the garbage can. The parents quietly and sadly looked on, not yet understanding. They had no hopes for their child. I then called a few of the faithful brethren who had real faith, and talked with them, reminding them of the incident when Christ went into the home of Jarius when his little daughter was lying apparently dead, and there with only a few of his faithful disciples, he raised her up and with this encouragement in our minds we went into definite fervent prayer. We cried out to God to confirm His Word with signs following, and He did that very thing. Yes, the prayers were truly fervent, and the answer came promptly. The child began to move its eyes, and then lifted one little hand, and moved its mouth. All present saw this, and began weeping and praising God aloud. God had worked in a mighty way—performing a miracle. Oh, glory to His Holy Name. The healing was done. As the Mother looked on she could hold out no longer, but broke down and fell on her knees and began calling on God to save her. She surrendered her life and all to him that day, and although a number of years have passed, she is still happily and faithfully serving the Lord Jesus. Glory to God in the highest; He is truly the very same yesterday, today and forever. His promises are unbreakable, we only need to believe.

From my heart I thank God for the day Sister E. Faith Stewart came to Cuba, bringing God's Eternal Standard of Truth, and teaching us of His divinely organized church. I thank Him that through this knowledge of His Divine Truth—He is my personal Saviour and Healer. And having had the privilege of living with Sister Stewart a few years, I have learned the true life of faith. Thank the Lord, in Him we live, and move and do have our being. We know that with Him nothing is impossible. Pray that I be always faithful.

Yours in His Great Love,

Signed: MARIA LUISA PAZ

Healed of the Effects of Measles

Little Linda June Hughes, two year old daughter of Mr. and Mrs. Noah Hughes of Muncie, Indiana, had the measles in April of 1949. She was practically over them, when a very severe cough settled down on her, and she would cough until she would vomit, and would at the same time burn with a hot fever. She was in a very bad condition. On Wednesday evening, April 27th, we were ready to go to Willard Street Church of God revival, where Brother Otho Decker was evangelist, when a telephone call came saying that little Linda was very sick. We immediately went to the home of Brother Hughes. Before going we called others and asked them to have special agreement in prayer at the Church that night.

On our arrival at Brother Hughes' home, we anointed the child according to James 5:14-15, and had definite prayer for her healing. She became easier for a little while and then became very sick again. Again we prayed and God gave help, but the enemy was not willing to let go, and kept bringing the affliction back. But each time after prayer she would sleep awhile, and get some rest. Then about 9:30 p. m., before leaving for home we prayed again, and she slept well until about 1 a. m., when she was so bad that Brother Hughes called us again for prayer. We at once went in prayer, and took a definite stand against the affliction and asked God to send His power and put an end to the trouble, and our blessed Lord answered and definitely healed the baby. The fever left at once, the cough ceased, and that was the end of the trouble. Praise God forever, it does pay to persevere in prayer till the power of the enemy is broken.

Signed: MRS. ELIZABETH VANNATER.

Boyce Hughes, age seven years, while at school one day had a very hard fall and deeply skinned his knee, and came home crying with pain. In a short time he had a fever, and red streaks ran out from the knee, and it hurt him clear up under his arm. He had sustained a bad injury. The parents called for prayer about 8 p. m. and we went right over and obeyed the Word of God, and had definite prayer for his healing, and after prayer he got up and walked out to the kitchen, and he rested well all night and the next morning he returned to his school, definitely healed by the hand of God. Oh, that men everywhere would learn to put their trust in the great God of the universe.

Signed: ELIZABETH VANNATER.

Various Cases of Healing in Our Own Family

As a family we have trusted God for all our healing for many years, and it is marvelous to so live that God who loves us, can really care for us in every way. Too many today live so much closer to the drug store, than they do to the Lord Jesus that it is no wonder they don't get healed by divine power. And many times people who profess to be saved look at us as if we were either an antique or a prehistoric animal of some kind, or something very peculiar if we tell them we are trusting God for healing our bodies. But to those of us who have learned to believe His Word, He is real, thank God, and His promises become a very part of our lives.

When our daughter was only seven years old she was healed of a very bad case of affected tonsils and adenoids. Each winter she had sore throat so much, and her nostrils would be so closed up with the adenoids that she could not breath at all with her mouth closed, but had to sleep with her mouth wide open. In 1921 a doctor told my sister that if something was not done (meaning if we did not have her operated on) little Gail would have a face deformity in less than five years, which would ruin her for life. But thank God He did not permit this doctor's statement to come true. We believed definitely that Christ shed His blood to heal our bodies as well as to save our souls, so we trusted Him right through it all. The following spring we took little Gail to the Anderson, Indiana, camp meeting, and there had her prayed for, and the dear Lord answered prayer. She began sleeping well with her mouth nicely closed, and never had tonsilitis any more. In fact, every symptom of the trouble was gone, and she was a well child. She is now the mother of three fine children and her face is perfectly normal.

When our son was seven months old he took very bad with pneumonia. All forenoon he lay unconscious in our arms. At noon we called our pastor, Brother H. F. Allen, to come to our home and pray for the child. He came with his wife and Sister West, out to our home in Gaston, Ind. At that time we attended services at Muncie, Indiana, where Brother Allen was pastor. The baby was old enough to know Brother Allen. As they came in for prayer, I laid the unconscious child in Sister Allen's arms, and Brother Allen anointed him according to the Word of the Lord, and we all agreed in prayer for the healing. Just as soon as prayer was ended, the baby opened his eyes and looked up at Brother Allen and smiled. He was definitely healed from that same hour. Our older son, Harold, was also healed of rupture when just a boy.

In the year of 1922, we were out in our car, and were stopped at a road side by a group of young people. They had pulled to the side of the road and stopped because one of their crowd, a young lady, had slumped down in the seat unconscious, and they thought she was dead; and they were so confused they did not know what to do. Husband said, "all we can do in a case like this is to pray," and one of these poor young people said, "Anything," so we went to the car and looked at her, and felt for her pulse, but we could neither see nor feel any signs of life. We did not know what had happened to her, and had no way of finding out there. But thank the dear Lord, again our Lord was master of the situation. We anointed her according to James 5:14-15, and offered fervent prayer for God to prove to these young people that He had power for all things. Immediately after prayer she opened her eyes and began speaking. She raised up, and was, as far as we could see, restored to normal health. Bless the Lord, oh my soul, and all that is within me, bless His Holy name.

In Heb. 13:8, the Word says, "Jesus Christ, the same yesterday, and today, and forever." And thank God, He is still manifesting His divine power wherever He finds faith. We love Him today with all our hearts and by His grace we mean to do our best in His service until He calls us to our reward above.

Signed: ELIZABETH VANNATER,
2707 North Walnut Street
Muncie, Indiana.

Healed In Both Soul and Body

For the glory of God and the encouragement of others who are suffering, I desire to give my testimony and recommend my great Physician. I was reared in a spiritualistic district and knew nothing of the blessed Gospel of Jesus Christ until God let me get so sorely afflicted that I had to leave my home and family and go into the city of Havana seeking physical help to save my life so I could live on for my family of a husband and five small children.

I lived in the Oriente, the last province to the East of Cuba. I was so sorely afflicted in various ways that at last my husband sent me to Havana to a specialist as other doctors had failed to help me. This doctor had been highly recommended, and I went in confidence, but after being examined for different afflictions I was told that one of my most serious afflictions was a serious infection of the blood. I returned to my home with different medical treatments the doctor had given me, and I faithfully followed his instructions, but got worse instead of better. With other things I developed a very serious infection of my left arm, from a bad injection. At last I was so bad my husband took me again to Havana, but to our disappointment the doctor in whom I had my confidence had left for the United States, I was so seriously ill, and this disappointment was great. I wept over it, but my good husband said not to be discouraged as we would find another just as good, and thank God, we did. I went in this condition to stay with a friend in Los Pinos, Havana and she lived just across the street from a mission. I had never heard the Gospel, but was attracted there, and went, and began learning about the Saviour of Men, and His wonderful power and love. At last I was more concerned about my soul than my body, although I knew I was in a critical condition, and was going to have to be operated on for my left arm. But I learned the way of salvation and soon was rejoicing in the forgiveness of sins. Then I learned that God could also heal my body, and as I put my confidence in Him, He sent His power on my body and healed me of ALL my afflictions. My blood was purified, and the infection of my arm was definitely healed. It was of a great size, but when God healed it, it went to normal and I had NO operation. I had all preparations made in the hospital for the operation, but God did the work perfectly, and I was made to walk the streets and praise God for His marvelous works. I soon returned to my family, and later some of the ministers visited my home bringing the blessed message of salvation to that place. Today I am just praising the dear Lord for the great blessings of salvation. What a wonderful savior and healer I have found in Jesus.

After being healed and saved I went across the city to visit in the congregation of the Church of God there, and to give my testimony in public for what great things the Lord had done for me. Now I am happy in my home in the country, doing my best to give the Light of the Gospel to my friends and neighbors. Pray for me.

Your sister in the Faith once delivered to the Saints.

Signed: Mrs. Flor Maria Perez de Cordaba.

Jesus Christ, the Same Yesterday, Today, and Forever.
Heb. 13:8

Yes, God can heal us if we trust Him. In the year of 1944, I was taken very ill at home in Bauta, Cuba. I was indeed very ill with very many complaints here and there, and fever. My family and many other friends insisted on me having a doctor, but I was saved and believed in trusting the Lord, and refused to have a doctor. Even though I refused, they went and brought one, seeing that my condition was so grave. When he came, he said I was a very sick person, and that besides the sickness I was very weak in body and must be built up. He left different kinds of medicines, and the members of my family insisted that I have some of it. I firmly refused to take any, and I made it clear that I was trusting alone in the Lord Jesus.

One Saturday, the Ladies' Missionary Group met there, and while they were singing the hymn, "How could I be sad, How could the clouds appear when Jesus is near" (translated from Spanish), my soul was lifted up and I began to grasp by faith what God had for me. I felt His mighty power flowing over my weak body and I was healed of all that sickness. How I did praise Him! They all rejoiced to see me the next night in my place preaching the message He had given me. May God help us to ever be faithful to Him and to trust Him at all times. Then we will have the joy at all times of feeling His divine touch on our bodies when we are in need of His help.

Another Healing of a More Serious Affliction

When I was just twenty-two years old, I was taken down with tuberculosis, and I was so bad that the family called a doctor again to examine me, and he said frankly that I could not possibly live more than six months, and that I might go much sooner than that. But, glory to God, I had my divine physician right with me, and He has a power that no doctor can understand. My case was one of tuberculosis in an advanced stage, where from the human viewpoint, there was no help for me. In other words death was staring me in the face, and was sure as could be. Men with all their science have not reached a place where they can conquer death. Blessed be the name of the Lord, He has conquered death and the grave, and in His resurrection power we may be healed and have our lives extended.

One day while I was very low my spiritual mother, Sister E. Faith Stewart, Missionary to Cuba, came to my room and was talking with me and reading from God's Word. She read to me Psalms 103, and when she got to the third verse "Who forgiveth all thine iniquities; who healeth all thy diseases," my faith was lifted right up, and I did believe for healing. I did believe the promises were made for me, and glory filled my soul. I knew then that all His promises were dependable, they were true, they were for me. Praise God He healed me that day, and by the end of the six months that were the full limit of time the doctor had given me to live, I left my home and went out to another place to give my definite testimony of the divine healing of that terrible disease—tuberculosis, and to exhort men and women to believe in God. May God help us to really trust Him and to confide in His Holy Word of Promise.

Today I am a married man with one child, and am blessed with health and strength as I labour among the people of this district, preaching the Word of God in its fullness and power to a lost people.

God has given me many souls for my hire, and we are filled with joy as we labour on in His Vineyard.

Yours in His Happy Service

Signed: PRUDENCIA LINARES, Pastor
Central Clia, Camaguey, Cuba

Healed of Cancer and Tumors

In the spring of 1948 I was in very poor health, and was constantly losing weight and had fever every day. I continually leaned on God for strength, but I steadily grew worse. A deep hurting in my side kept me awake at nights. At last I decided to go to a doctor to find out just what my trouble was. He examined me thoroughly and then told me I had one tumor as large as a grapefruit and had some smaller ones around that one. He also said one of them seemed to be an active cancer and that I must be operated on without a day's delay.

I can never explain what my feelings were when told my condition, especially to be told I had a cancer. My grandmother, my own mother, and also one of my brothers had all died with that dread disease and I had a sister who was then past human help. I said, "Oh, God this just cannot happen to me. That doctor just must be mistaken. I will go to another and see what he says about my condition." Yet in my heart I knew it was. I have four sons and a husband who needed me badly. God had healed in our home many times, but this time it was hard to get the victory over this awful affliction. The scripture, "Fear not, I will be with thee," kept coming over and over in my mind. As the weeks passed by I knew this was something I alone would have to decide. I kept asking myself the question, "Does my faith take it in?" The more I prayed the more I knew Jesus wanted to heal me. And thank God the time came when I was ready to let Him do it. On the last day of February I had taken my bed, too sick to stay up longer. I asked my husband to call our pastor, Brother H. F. Allen, and three other faithful brethren of the congregation of the Willard Street Church of God, Muncie, Indiana, to come over and pray for my healing. They came and prayed the prayer of faith for me, and praise God, He healed me even before they had finished praying.

One week later I went to one of the same doctors, but this time just to prove to the people that I had really been healed. The docor said there was no signs of the cancer or the tumors. They were all gone—glory be to God forever. Oh, how can we ever doubt Him?

One year before this I was in a car accident, and my right arm was badly injured and my left foot was so badly broken that I was led to believe I might never walk on that foot again. This was in September, but I trusted God, and in December I did all my Christmas shopping without the aid of my crutch. God so answered prayer, that a few months later when we had the foot X-rayed again, the X-ray showed the bones were perfect.

In the year 1947 our seven year old son, Warren, was instantly healed of rheumatic fever. Again in 1948 this same child was instantly healed of virus disease. In each case the church prayed earnestly and prayer was answered. I love my dear Lord with all my heart. He has saved my soul and healed my body. I entreat you, do not be afraid to trust Him for whatever you may need.

Signed: LOLA A. ROOCH
224 East 8th Street
Muncie, Indiana

CHAPTER X

God's Protecting Care

Great and Mighty Are His Works

The psalmist, David, had some glorious experiences with God, and these enlarged his vision of God's greatness and all through his writings, he cried out of the depth of his soul, magnifying God for His mighty works to the children of men. In Psalms 40:4 he exclaimed "Blessed is that man that maketh the Lord his trust" and in verse 5, "Many, O Lord, my God, are thy wonderful works which Thou hast done and Thy thoughts which are to us-ward: they cannot be reckoned up in order unto thee: if I would declare and speak of them, they are more than can be numbered." How true these works are. His thoughts toward His true children are very great. His blessings to us are more than can be numbered. Praise His worthy name.

About the middle of January 1935, I had a very marvelous experience with the Lord which I here relate, trusting it may help others to "hide away in His pavilion" and to learn some of the "secrets of the Lord." I arose in the morning with a full day planned in active service for my Master. Soon, a heavy burden so fully enveloped my soul that I could do nothing but pray. At different times during the day I left my room to start out to do some of the many things that were awaiting me, but each time I would attempt to leave the house the same overwhelming burden would come back, and I would come back, and I would be forced by the promptings of the Spirit of God to return to the secret place of prayer. Thus the hours of the day passed away. That night, I went to the church service and there I told of my burden and asked the brethren to pray that God would lift the burden so I could deliver the message of Truth He had laid on my heart. They got under the burden and prayed very earnestly, and the dear Lord did liberate me so I could preach, but as soon as the service was over, the weight again came on my soul and I wept and prayed until 1:30 in the morning when the crushing burden was not only lifted but a full assurance was given that whatever was before me, God would be with me and care for me. Sweet peace then filled my soul and I slept like a child until about 4 a. m. when something suddenly awakened me and in a moment I was confronted by two armed men—one with a revolver and the other with a long knife which is used much in Cuba as a weapon. I definitely heard voices in other rooms and knew well that a group of armed bandits had entered to rob and to kill. But in this same moment, a voice spoke to me out of heaven, in unmistakably clear words, and saying "The angel of the Lord encampeth round about them that fear him, and delivereth them" Ps. 34:7. Praise our God! My heart was calm; my soul at ease; God was there.

Before entering the home, these men had bored a hole in the kitchen door and had inserted a funnel and through that, had blown in gas—and with us all under gas, they had entered and had done a complete job of robbing the home of all valuables—silverware, linens, bedding, clothing and all office supplies. I was bodily thrown from one part of the bed to another and kept where they put me, with the knife and revolver held over me. When they were convinced that nothing of value was left, they went out to their well-loaded car and drove away. In the room next to me were two young ladies (students in the Bible Training School) and one small girl. These men were definitely searching for money and not finding what satisfied them, they repeatedly declared that if they did not get what they wanted they would kill me. Although their weapons were raised in anger at me several times, God did not permit any one of us to be harmed. As soon as they departed and the alarm could be given, neighbors rushed in, and the first ones who entered threw up their hands with an exclamation of horror, and brought a looking glass for me to see my white hair that had changed color in less than one hour. Policemen, detectives and American officials rushed in and none could understand how we had escaped death. This took place in the time of the Machado Revolution and the American officials told us that in that same week, in that same part of the city, burglars had entered eight other homes, and that in each of these, from one to three persons had been left dead. And in our home no one was injured in any way. Oh, how marvelous are His works toward them that fear Him. Yes, "the Angel of the Lord encampeth round about them that fear Him and delivereth them."

God never does fail those who love and serve Him, with true hearts. He has been with us in the past and will be with us to the end. "Draw nigh unto the Lord and He will draw nigh unto thee." But dear reader, we cannot live afar off from the Lord, and follow our own ways and expect Him to be with us in times of trouble. Let us delight ourselves in the way of the Lord, and He shall direct our paths, and overshadow us with His Love.

Safe In His Keeping

Experiences With Communists

"When a man's ways please the Lord, He maketh even his enemies to be at peace with him." Proverbs 16:7. This scripture is as true as any other, and we are safe in expecting a fulfillment of its promise IF OUR WAYS DO PLEASE THE LORD.

Early in the year of 1947, I had a strange experience in that each night when I had to go over to the other side of the city for a service in the church, near the close of the meeting I would notice a brother from the Children's Homes entering the meeting and quietly taking a seat. I did not think so much about it when we were in a Spanish service, but when the same thing happened the night of the service for the English speaking brethren, I did look on in amazement, as this brother did not understand any English and had never before attended these services. But each time when I would ask why he had come, he would just quietly say, "I came over to accompany you in going home." I was troubled at this act, for it had never been done before, but I said little as I knew how very kind this brother was, and did not want to discourage him. After this had continued some six weeks, I learned why it was done. One afternoon a "Chief-of-police" came to the door at the HOME and asked the privilege of speaking privately with me. I took him into the office, and after carefully closing all the windows, he turned to me and asked if there was anyone in hearing distance. I told him I felt sure there was not, and then he told me he had come to bring secret information. That the communists had a plot—and it included killing me and the very same brother who had been coming over to the church so I would not have to go home alone. That it also included the destruction of both our Children's Homes. He said he had known something of the plan for some time, but had waited until he had full proof before alarming me. But that he could not keep it from me longer. He said he did not know what method they planned on using to destroy the work of the Children's Homes, but that it was a definite plot, to be put in action. He warned me never to leave the Homes alone, and never to return from any place late at night. That if it was absolutely necessary to go out, to remain away until the next day—and then to return under protection. After he left I called Brother Morales in (the one who had been watching for my protection), and told him, and to my great astonishment he told me that he had known all this for six weeks. It was for that reason he had been following, trying to give protection, but he did not want to tell me what was hanging over us.

Shortly before this we had learned that the Communistic Training School for Cuba was located next door to our Boy's Home. We had been told by many that there was some kind of a Men's Club there, but no one seemed to know that it was this Training School. On the other side of us, just one block from the Homes was the bus terminal for the suburb of Los Pinos where I then lived. All of the employees of that bus company were communists. When fully awake to the danger that surrounded us, we called the faithful brethren together and let them know the plot of these enemies. Oh, how faithful our brethren were both in prayer and in their attention in those days of danger. Day after day some of them came early in the morning, staying all day, sitting on the verandahs, or walking around the buildings, just to be there with us. What a strength we felt from their presence, and from their prayers. At last—early one morning a group of some twenty men marched into the front yard, and right upon the verandah of the missionary department, and there raising their hands heavenward—they denounced the HOMES in terms strong and ugly. They had with them then, two of our precious little children that they had already kidnapped. After denouncing the HOMES they turned and rushed off. What could we do—notify the police—ah, no, for one police was right with them. All we could do was to call on God. Some of the workers did rush off to the police station, but these men were there before our brethren could get there, and had turned in a false report to condemn the HOMES. We were in the hands of our's and Christ's enemies—the communists. And before night of that day they had kidnapped four of our darling little children. The next Sunday—the Communist publication, "Hoy" had a large picture of this group of men with the first two children they had taken; and the HOMES were denounced in strong terms, in large letters. Our sky grew darker with the passing hours, and our only comfort was that we knew that "underneath were the Everlasting Arms of Our Blessed Lord and Saviour." Praise our God forever.

Four days later another group came in a large car with a loud speaker on top. They entered the Boy's Home and were trying to break down some doors, when we stopped them to await the keys. On entering the rooms they found nothing but clean well ordered rooms, with the doors closed to keep the children out of the rooms until time to enter for their clothes for bathing. Then these seven men went around onto the verandah of the Missionary department and sat down, talking in loud voices, and again denouncing the HOMES, and declaring they were going to destroy those Institutions. We had to go to the American officials for advice and protection, and had to get a lawyer to defend our case, as they had a case in court against us. And we soon learned that our money for the lawyer was lost, and he was afraid to defend us, as he knew what the cost would be to him. At last we found out clearly that we had no defense from a human standpoint as all were afraid, so the church just kept crying out to God, and day after day we had His mighty protection on all sides. Oh glory be to His matchless name. At this same time a group of these men entered a man's home to kill him, and finding him out, they killed his young wife and shot through the baby, and this infant died a few days later in the hospital. What tragedies we were then surrounded with—but the Church Prayed—and God continued to protect us. Several months of this suffering passed. We lost, in all, ten of our precious children, and had most of our activities in the city curbed, but as the Church prayed, God stayed the hand of the enemy.

The year ended with the shadow still over us, but we kept on doing all possible for souls, and trusted God to bring victory. He brought it in even a fuller sense than we had expected. Early in January, a telephone call came from the home of the communists, saying the School of Instructions was closed, and the students and teachers gone. They were selling off everything—furniture, bedding, etc., as fast as possible, to clear things out. They thought since we had an institution (which they had not had power to destroy—thank God) we might like to buy some things, and if so, to go over and have first choice of the things. A group of us went over, and we bought enough three-decker beds for our Boy's Home, and a lot of blankets, mattresses, etc., for a very low price. We also bought some other much needed pieces of furniture. As we returned home we called all the children and workers of the Homes together to see what great things God had done for us. THE COMMUNISTIC TRAINING SCHOOL WAS GONE—THANK GOD FOR ANSWERED PRAYER. Then on the 9th of February we were talking about the ANNIVERSARY of the Homes which would be the next day. Formerly this was a happy day for all, but because of the tremendous cloud that had hung over us so long, and the heavy expenses it had brought on us, we had made NO preparations for the day. We were talking about this when the phone rang and someone went to answer, and returned saying the call was from a watchman over at that school, and that they had remembered the date of the opening of Our Homes, and wondered if we would not like to take the children and workers all over to that place and let them have a good time playing on the grounds there. They had wonderful grounds, and also the dining hall was still all intact, as the furniture had not been sold. We considered it, and accepted the invitation. We called the teachers whom the government sends us daily and invited them, and also a number of our ministers and other brethren, and we all went over and had the joy of triumphing over our foes. As we sat down to eat dinner we asked the four who were living on the premises to care for things there, to eat with us, and these poor souls for the first time in their lives had to bow their heads with us as we thanked God for the beautiful day, and the good food, and the kindness of those who had given us the privilege of using those grounds. And we prayed for God to bless them, and teach them His will. The day closed with many blessings to all. Praise God, "If our ways please the Lord, He maketh even our enemies to be at peace with us." I might just say that the Lord also cleaned out the communist employees from the bus company, and gave victory. And now in the place of the school, we have the comfort of having a good dairy farm there, run by quiet people. Praise God from whom all blessings flow!

"The eyes of the Lord run to and fro throughout the whole earth, to shew Himself strong in behalf of those whose hearts are perfect towards Him."
II Chron. 16:9

Some years ago while I was working in Missionary work in Cuttack, India, we had a wonderful demonstration of the fulfillment of this great promise, which I shall relate here.

Our Church of God camp meeting had ended (in Cuttack) and the brethren from various parts of India were returning to their different fields of labour. A few of the ministers had remained over a day or two after the departure of the others, to talk together and plan some of the activities in their special fields. The day of departure of these brethren had come. One of this group had been very seriously ill for some time, and had been brought to the camp meeting with great care, but trying to get him there for the benefit of united prayer. God had definitely touched his body, and he was gaining rapidly, but was still in a very weak condition, so it was planned that this good brother must be taken back to his home (a full night's journey) in a good compartment on the train, so he could have some rest, and also not to endanger his health again. The compartment was arranged for, and paid for in plenty of time to secure reservation. The other brethren would go in the same compartment, although they had no bed.

The morning of the day of their departure arrived, and that morning all the group who were going had a very unusual burden come on their hearts; and so did those of us who were remaining behind. So we prayed very earnestly, asking God to take care of everything for us. They started at midday, and had only gone a short distance in the coach, till this burden so increased that they told the driver to return to the mission house, which he did. As we saw them returning our burden increased the more, and we all entered again into deep prayer. They said they just could not understand their feelings—but after much prayer, they again left for the station. As they reached there and went to enter the coach assigned to them, to their amazement they found it completely full, and the passengers showed by their tickets that they had a right to the compartment. These passengers had entered the train farther down the line, and then we learned that the agent at Cuttack had no notice of these passengers and was not at fault. We knew that nothing could be done about this situation, so all our brethren could do was to enter a THIRD class compartment, which offered very bad accommodations for the sick brother. They committed it all to the Lord, and started their homeward journey. Being much worn from the heavy work of the camp meeting, they were soon all asleep in spite of poor accommodations, and knew nothing more until one brother awoke hearing voices. Putting his head out of an open window, he asked someone standing there where they were. The man was surprised, and answered, "Man, where have you been? Sleeping through all this?" The brother then asked, "Sleeping through all of WHAT?" Then the answer came back,

"We have collided with another train, and many are killed, and scores of people injured." What a shock! What an awakening to the great providence of God, and what a surge of gratitude filled our brethren's hearts, to know God had spared them. Not a scar, not a bruise. As the ones who were well rushed out of their compartment to offer what assistance they might be able to render, they discovered that the compartment in which they should have traveled, was smashed to pieces, and not a passenger in that compartment was alive. With sad hearts at what they witnessed, but with hearts melted before God as they looked on His great power in saving them, they bowed in grateful praise to Him who was worthy. They knew they were alive ONLY BECAUSE OF THE GREAT INTERVENTION OF THEIR HEAVENLY FATHER. Yes, the eyes of the Lord do run to and fro throughout the whole earth, to show himself strong in behalf of those whose hearts are perfect towards Him. Bless His dear Holy name forever and forever.

Brethren, it pays to so live in touch with the throne of God that at any time when in danger, He can send His Holy Spirit to direct us, and to guide and to warn, and to prepare us for His own intervention, that we may be protected and helped through the coming danger. Let us love Him sincerely and trust in Him fully, and He will never fail us.

"Ye have seen that I have talked with you from heaven"
Exodus 20:22

In 1932, I was working at my office desk in my home in Buena Vista, Havana, when I heard a knock at the front door, and naturally put my work aside, and arose to open the door. My desk was in the room just back of the living room, and a heavy curtain hung between the two rooms. Just as I arose from the chair, a voice spoke to me directly, saying, "Do not invite that person in, but open the door, and pass out to the verandah." The voice was so clear that at once I recognized it as the voice of the Lord, and definitely obeyed it.

As I raised the curtain to step out, I saw a man standing there who was an enemy of the TRUTH, and with whom I had had some dealing, and I knew him to be capable of doing harm. He was a strong Catholic and was very bitter against us and our work.

On reaching the front door, I did exactly what the Spirit of God had told me to do, I opened the screen door, and immediately stepped out on the verandah. As I did this, I saw neighbors sitting out on their verandahs, both at the side of my house, and also across the street. Naturally this poor man was surprised, and angered, for he had a revolver in his pocket to kill me with and had not expected a defeat like this was. He knew both languages, English and Spanish, and knowing that the neighbors were all Spanish speaking, he spoke to me in English. In great anger he said he had come to kill me, and that he would yet accomplish it if it was the last thing he ever did. I quietly stayed outside until his anger cooled a bit and he left. One of the neighbors saw the revolver and reported it, and the police gave him warning, and watched for some days. The church prayed for God to take care of the whole thing, which He did, soon removing this man to another country in his work. Thank God, again I was made to realize more than ever how marvelous are the ways of the Lord.

In Exodus 20:22 we read, "Ye have seen that I have talked with you from heaven," and although God was there speaking to Moses, He still speaks to His trusting children and guides them, and saves them from the hand of their enemies, and proves that He was not only the God of the Israelites, but that in a very definite way HE IS OUR GOD—and He does care for us at all times. In olden times God made a promise with the children of Israel that if they should forsake all else, and cleave to Him and obey ALL His commandments and keep ALL His Statutes, He would *then* be their God, and would care for them. And for us today— He has made the same promise—that if we keep His commandments, AND DO THOSE THINGS THAT ARE PLEASING IN HIS SIGHT, I John 4:22—He will be with us, and answer our prayers and keep us. His eyes are on the sparrow, and he sees it's fall—then how much more will He care for those who really love and serve Him wholeheartedly. Praise the Lord.

These experiences, that I am writing about in this book are not ordinary experiences that come to the cold professor of religion, or that come in the life of the careless Christian. If we desire God's protecting care, we must by our devotions and our consecration prove to Him that we are His indeed and that our lives are really to be poured out for His glory. But with this close, devoted living, there comes into the life a depth of spirituality that keeps the soul in vital touch with heaven, and it is then easy to hear from above when the need comes upon us. Thank God for His wonderful plan for us. Let us live worthily, and reach out more and more for that intimate life with our Lord that assures us of His constant companionship in life.

CHAPTER XI

Suggestive Helps To A Life Of Faith

Although this book is not a treatise on divine healing for the body, still God's promises do cover this physical need the same as they cover all other needs in this life. If we are definitely Christ's through salvation from sin, through the atonement of Calvary, we are then His in a two-fold sense. 1. Through creation we are God's, we belong to Him in a definite way, for He made us. 2. After the fall of man in the garden of Eden, God put into action His great plan for the Eternal redemption of mankind, and thus purchased us back through the great sacrifice of His Only Son. So according to I Cor. 6:19-20, we belong to God both soul and body. Here Paul said, "What? know ye not that your body is the temple of the Holy Ghost which is in you, which ye have of God and ye are not your own? For ye are bought with a price: therefore, glorify God in your body, and in your spirit, which are God's." Yes, we are bought with a great price—bought with the precious blood of Christ. "For as much as ye know that ye are not redeemed with corruptible things as silver and gold—but with the precious blood of Christ." I Peter 18-19.

God's plan of redemption covers a complete work—a full restoration. The soul is restored into a relationship with the Father as soon as the individual definitely accepts the divine plan of God for his salvation. He then becomes a partaker spiritually of the divine nature. Read II Peter 1:3-4. Then, thank God, as long as we walk in the light of His Word, we are kept in His likeness. Praise God forever for His marvelous plan. Our eternal redemption is then for us sure—*just as long as we live in definite obedience* to all the light we have on His Holy Word.

And although our physical redemption is not yet complete, and will not be until "the last enemy (death) is destroyed," and "this mortal shall have put on immortality," still God has not forgotten our physical needs and He has planned to care for these mortal bodies (which have, through His plan, become the temple of the Holy Spirit) UNTIL the glorious triumph of the final resurrection. Yes, He has planned to care for the bodies of His children by stretching forth His hand of power to heal their bodily afflictions. His Holy Word is full of definite promises for His children. He first made known this part of His plan when He declared to the Israelites, "I am the Lord that healeth thee." Ex. 15:26. And thank the Lord, from that day to this he has healed those who live for Him, and trust in His Work of promise. Divine healing for the body is a sort of forerunner of immortality. The "will" of God in this respect is well expressed in the desire of the beloved Apostle John when he said, "Beloved, I wish above all things that thou mayest prosper and be in health, even as thy soul prospereth." 3 John 2. I am aware that the blessed doctrine of divine healing for the body has been ignored by many, but, "What if some do not believe? Shall their unbelief make the promises of God without effect?" (for those who do believe). What people believe or do not believe does not settle the great facts of TRUTH, but it is what the Word says on the subject.

God was the healer of His children, the Israelites; and the Prophets of old predicted a special manifestation of His healing power when Christ should come. The Prophet Isaiah speaking of the coming of the Lord said, "He would be a light to the Gentiles" and that he should "open the eyes of the blind." Isa. 42:7. Christ, preaching in the synagogue of Nazareth said, "This day is this scripture fulfilled in your ears" Luke 4:18-21. Again in Isa. 35:4-6 we read, "Say to them that are of a fearful heart—be strong, fear not; behold your God will come with vengeance, even God with a recompense; He will come and save you. THEN the eyes of the blind shall be opened, and the ears of the deaf shall be unstopped. THEN shall the lame man leap as an hart and the tongue of the dumb shall sing." Isa. 35:4-6. The Prophet Malachi also predicted the healing work of Christ, "but unto you that fear my name shall the Sun of Righteousness arise with healing in His wings." Mal. 4:2. Thank God, all these were fulfilled in the coming of Christ and, "He is just the same today." Hebrews 13:8. It is only for us to refuse to give any place to doubts and unbelief, and to stand firmly on His Word of Promise, remembering always that these bodies of ours (if we are redeemed) ARE THE TEMPLES OF THE HOLY GHOST and He surely will care for His own.

What is needed today is men and women who are decided in their hearts to lift up God's standard of Divine Truth for His own glory. Paul said in Heb. 11:6, "But without faith it is impossible to please God, for he that cometh to God must believe that He is, and that He is a rewarder of them that diligently seek Him." What a message of Truth these few words bring to our hearts. Yes, we cannot get anything from God, in answer to prayer, UNLESS we definitely believe—FIRST—that He is—that He exists, and then more than that, we must believe that if we diligently seek ANYTHING from Him, (in faith) He will give it to us. Without this faith, it is impossible to PLEASE GOD—so knowing this, how diligently we should seek an increase of faith, so our lives may please Him. Let us be strong in the faith that was once delivered to the saints. If you are a minister of the gospel of Christ, one very definite part of your commission is to be able to pray the prayer of faith for the healing of the sick. And if you are just a believer—just a little member in the body of Christ (which IS His church) still Jesus has said to you, "These signs shall follow them that believe—," and also He said, "believers shall lay hands on the sick, and they shall recover." Mark 16:18.

In this day of Communism, of Atheism, and of unbelief, God's children everywhere need to arise and shake themselves, and step forward as never before, determined that the world shall see the church shining forth in all her beauty and glory just as in the morning time, with mighty signs and wonders following the preaching of the Word, and the labors of His present day disciples. Then and then only will the world around us look on and believe, and be brought to the cross for salvation. The conversion of thousands followed the healings and other demonstrations of God's power working among His people in the morning time church, and the same results would follow today, if we were a clear demonstration of the same mighty working power. Jesus said, "and I, if I be lifted up (through Godly lives, and through signs following) will draw all men unto me." Then why so much unbelief in the world today? Because the signs are not following in many places as they should be in a normal church of God. Let us awaken and live it, and preach it, and see the results.

How Can We Have the Faith?

Paul said, after a long life of rich experiences with the Lord, "faith cometh by hearing, and hearing by the word of God" Rom. 10:17. Yes, hearing the preaching of the Word on these lines will edify and build up our faith. And a personal study of God's promises on the subject of faith or of His dealings with His faithful children in ages past, coupled with a careful study of His promises for the present and the future will build up our faith and bring it to a point of activity. Passive faith brings but little to the life of man, but a definite, active, living faith moving out on the promises of God and taking from Him by FAITH just what He has promised to us—brings the needed help on any line, and also builds us up for greater ventures of faith in the future.

If one desires to "live a life of faith," desires to be used of God as a channel of blessing to others, it is absolutely necessary to have a humble heart, free from all pride—for God knoweth the proud afar off. It is necessary to have a daily walk with God in obedience to His Word and Will for us. The WRITTEN WORD of God is a clear expression of His divine WILL or PLAN for the life of ALL His children. A careful study of His Word with a sincere desire to know His full will for us, so that plan may be lived right out in our daily lives, brings us on "praying ground" where our faith can then take hold of His promises of God and make them real in our lives. Praying the effectual prayer of the righteous— brings the answer.

Also, aside from God's universal or general plan for all His children, as set forth in His Word (as a lamp to our feet, and a guide to our pathway) He has also His own plan for each individual life in our service to Him, and this will all be clearly made known to us, if we commit all our ways unto Him, and give Him the privilege of directing our lives. Prov. 3:5-6. The wonderful promises of God are for those who love and obey Him, and let Him have His own way in their lives. In St. John 15:7, we read, "If ye abide in me, and my words abide in you, *ye shall ask what ye will, and it shall be done unto you.*" Praise God for such a mighty promise. Ask *what* ye will, and it shall be done unto you. This promise covers not only the healing of the body, but also the supply of all our material needs, and all our spiritual needs. But this promise is conditional—"If ye abide in me (a settled, steadfast Christian life), and if my Words abide in you (a life lived in harmony to the whole word of

God) THEN—THEN—ask, and receive. Praise the Lord. This scripture lays down the full condition, and the promise covers our every need in life. Then let us see to it that our lives are up to the full standard of Truth and then let us exercise ourselves in a deep prayer life, and the joy of answered prayer may be our daily portion. To live a life of faith we must have a heart free from all pride, and be clothed with humility; to live a life of faith we must be definitely separated from the world and separated unto the LORD; to see the results of faith in our lives, we must so live that it is easy to touch the throne of God, and bring the answer down. THERE IS A PRICE TO PAY if we want to be able to bless the world by the effectual prayer of the righteous being fruitful in our own lives. Let us not "play" Christian—but let us settle down in Him, take Him at His Word, and then, and then only can the world around us be blessed by Christ in His Power having been lifted up—and sinners will be drawn to the cross. When Jesus was on earth, and following His ministry, while the early morning church was shining out in her beauty and glory, multitudes of men and women were added to the Church, through the powerful demonstrations of God's power working among them. It should and would be the same today, if only the redeemed of the Lord would so live that the "signs and wonders" would follow the ministry of the Word. This brings a great responsibility on each child of God. Let us arise, and go forth in His name, proving to the non-Christian world around us that Jesus still lives today—in His People, and that "He is the very same—yesterday, today and forever."

Most of the world is still lost and in darkness—WHY?—because Jesus, The Christ of God, The Saviour from all sin, the healer of all sicknesses, the Friend of mankind, the supplier of our needs—Jesus—The Son of God—*has not been lifted up.* He has been over-shadowed by a great cloud of unbelief, and doubts and fears. A formal religion *will not* draw men—a cold profession *will not* draw men—programmes and entertainment *will not* draw men—but a good, clear demonstration of WHAT CHRIST is, and what He WILL be to those who trust Him, WILL draw men unto Him. Brother—sister— *"What is that—thou hast in thy hand?"* Ex. 4:2. The *powerful gospel of the Son of God. This is what men need,* and want—let us go forth without fear, giving them what we have received. "Freely ye have received, freely give." Jesus said, "Heal the sick, cleanse the lepers, raise the dead, cast out devils; freely ye have received, freely give." Matt. 10:8. God bless every reader. Amen.

CHAPTER XII

Miraculous Events On Record
In The Holy Scriptures

The creation of the world—Gen. 1:1-31.

The creation of man—Gen. 2:7.

Woman made from the rib of man—Gen. 2:21-24.

Enoch's translation—Gen. 5:24 and Heb. 11:5.

The Deluge—Gen. 7:1-24.

The miraculous confusion of tongues—Gen. 11:1-9.

The destruction of Sodom and Gomorrah—Gen. 19:23-28.

The burning bush—Exodus 3:2.

God sends food from heaven for His children—Ex. 16:4-25.

The leprosy of Miriam—Numbers 12:9-10 and Deut. 24:9.

The ass speaks to Balaam—Num. 22:22-35.

The slaying of the Philistines before the ark—I Sam. 5:1-12; 6:1-21.

Ussah killed by touching God's Ark—2 Sam. 6:6-7.

The hand of Jeroboam withered—1 Kings Sam.13:4-6.

The translation of Elijah—2 Kings 2:11.

Water provided for Jehosaphat's army—2 Kings 3:16-20.

The Hebrew children preserved in the furnace—Dan. 3:19-27.

Daniel's life preserved in the den of lions—Dan. 6:16-23.

Jonah lives three days in the belly of the whale—Jonah 2:1-10.

The Immaculate conception of Christ—Matt. 1:18, Luke 1:27-35.

The Spirit like a dove descending at the baptism of Christ—Matt. 3:16, Mark 10:1.

The resurrection of Christ—Matt. 28:6, Mark 16:6, Luke 24:6, John 26:17.
Tongues given at Pentecost—Acts 2:4.
Prison doors opened, bands loosened—Acts 16:25-40.

The above mentioned events were wrought directly through the hand of God, and now we shall cite a number where God worked through some of His servants to accomplish Miracles and Healings.

Abraham
Abimelech healed through Abraham's prayers—Gen. 20:17.
Son given in old age, by faith—Rom. 4:13-25, Gen. 17:16-19, Gen. 21:1-5.
The sacrifice furnished at the offering of Isaac—Gen. 22:8-13.

Moses and Aaron
A rod turned into a serpent—Exodus 4:3 and 7:10.
The ten plagues of Egypt—Exodus 7:20, 10:23.
The parting of the waters of the Red Sea—Exodus 14:6-31.
Water sweetened at Marah—Exodus 15:25.
Water from the rock—Exodus 17:5-7.
Miriam healed of leprosy—Number 12:13-15.

Joshua
Waters of Jordan divided—Josh. 3:10-17.
Destruction of Jericho—Josh. 6:6-20.
The sun and moon stayed—Josh. 10:12-14.

Samuel
Thunder and rain sent—1 Sam. 12:18.

The Prophet of Judah
Healing of king's hand—1 Kings 13:6.

Elijah
Drought caused—1 Kings 17:1; James 5:17.
The widow's meal increased—1 Kings 17:14-16.
The widow's son raised from the dead—1 Kings 17: 17-24.
Sacrifice consumed by fire from heaven—1 Kings 18: 30-38.

Rain sent in answer to prayer—1 Kings 18:41, James 5:18.
Waters of Jordan divided—2 Kings 2:8.

Elisha

The river Jordan divided—2 Kings 2:14.
A spring of water healed through prayer—2 Kings 2:21-22.
Oil multiplied—2 Kings 4:1-7.
Shunammite's son restored to life—2 Kings 4:32-37.
One hundred men fed with twenty loaves—2 Kings 4:42-44.
Naaman healed of leprosy—2 Kings 5:1-14.
Syrians smitten with blindness—2 Kings 6:18.
Syrians' sight restored—2 Kings 6:20.
A man restored to life—2 Kings 13:21.

Isaiah

Healing of King Hezekiah—2 Kings 20:7.
The dial turns backward—2 Kings 20:11.

Miracles and Healing by Jesus Christ

Healing of all manner of sickness and disease—Matt. 4:23-24.
Cleansing of leper—Matt. 8:1-4.
Centurian's servant healed—Matt. 8:5-13, and Luke 7:1-10.
Healing of Peter's wife's mother—Matt. 8:14-15, Luke 4:38-39.
Devils cast out of many—Matt. 8:16.
The tempest stilled—Matt. 8:23-27, Mark 4:36-41.
Devils cast into swine—Matt. 8:28-34.
Palsied man healed—Matt. 9:1-8, Luke 5:18-26.
Woman healed just by touching the hem of His garment—Matt. 9:20-22, Luke 8:43-48.
Jairus' daughter brought back to life—Matt. 9:23-25, Mark 5:22-42.
Two blind men restored—Matt. 9:27-31.
Withered hand restored—Matt. 12:10-13, Mark 3:1-5.
Jesus walks on the Sea—Matt. 14:22-31.
Feeding of five thousand—Matt. 15:21, John 6:5-13.
Four thousand fed—Matt. 15:32-39, Mark 8:1-9.
Blind, dumb, lame healed—Matt. 15:30.
A fish caught with tribute money—Matt. 17:24-27.
The cursing of the fig tree—Matt. 21:18-22.
A blind man healed—Mark 8:22-26.

Jesus escapes unseen from his pursuers—Luke 4:30.
The miraculous draught of fishes—Luke 5:1-11.
Young man raised from dead—Luke 7:11-17.
Woman healed of infirmity—Luke 13:10-17.
Ten lepers healed—Luke 17:11-19.
Servant's ear cut off, then restored—Luke 22:50-51.
Water turned into wine—John 2:1-11.
Nobleman's son healed—John 4:46-54.
Impotent man at the Pool of Bethesda—John 5:1-16.
Man, blind from birth, healed—John 9:1-41.
The raising of Lazarus—John 11:1-46.

Miracles and Healings by the Hand of the Apostles
They cast out devils—Mark 6:13.
They anointed and healed the sick—Mark 6:13.
The preaching was confirmed by "signs following"—Mark 16:20.
Signs and wonders were done—Acts 2:43.
Wonders wrought by their hands in Iconium—Acts 14:3-4.
Many sick healed in the streets of Jerusalem—Acts 5:12-16.

The Seventy were sent out to PREACH and HEAL
Had the power to heal the sick and to cast out devils—Luke 10:9-20.

Peter
Lame man healed—Acts 3:7.
Death of Ananias and Sapphira—Acts 5:5-10.
Many sick healed—Acts 5:15-16.
Dorcas restored to life—Acts 9:40.

Stephen
Great wonders and miracles done by him—Acts 6:8.

Ananias
Laid his hands on Saul that he might receive his sight—Acts 9:17-18.

Philip
Miracles and signs—Acts 8:13.
The lame and palsied healed—Acts 8:7.
Performed miracles before the people—Acts 8:6-7.

Paul

Spirit of divination cast out—Acts 16:16-18.

Lame man healed—Acts 14:8-10.

Holy Ghost and tongues given by the laying on of hands—Acts 19:6.

Handkerchiefs and aprons sent—Acts 19:11-12.

Eutychus restored to life—Acts 20:10-12.

Paul saved from harm when bitten by a viper—Acts 28:5.

The Church at Jerusalem

Peter delivered from prison through the prayers of the church—Acts 2:5-17.

There are also counterfeit healings and miracles done by the devil to deceive the people.

Here we cite a few miracles done through evil agents:

Signs and lying wonders—2 Thess. 2:9.

Spirits of devils working miracles—Rev. 16:14.

Signs or wonders in support of false religions—Deut. 13:1-5.

Great signs and wonders by false Christs—Matt. 24:24

Miracles wrought by false prophets—Rev. 19:20.

Signs and wonders by false prophets—Matt. 24:24.

Power to make fire come down from heaven—Rev. 13:13.

Power to work miracles and to deceive the people—Rev. 13:14.

Magicians' rods become serpents—Exodus 7:12.

Water of river turned to blood by enchantment of magicians—Exodus 7:22.

Frogs brought up by enchantment—Exodus 8:7.

Simon the sorcerer bewitched the people—Acts 8:9-24

Let us as children of God learn to try the spirits, that we be not deceived and seek our help in times of sickness or other needs, from God alone. Read 1 John 4:1, "Beloved, believe not every spirit, but try the spirits whether they be of God: because MANY FALSE PROPHETS have gone out into the world." Yes, today the religious world is filled with false prophets who are going about working all kinds of miracles, and deceiving the people. It is alarming to see how even the true saints of God will run after these and believe in their works. We often hear this remark, "but they are doing such mighty healings, etc., SURELY they are of God." Again I warn you, TRY THE SPIRITS—whether they be of

God—yes, try them by God's own word. The doctrine they teach, and the lives they live will soon tell whether they are of God. But let us not cast away our confidence in God because of the workings of these "false prophets" but let us plant our spiritual feet on the ETERNAL ROCK OF DIVINE TRUTH, and move forward in a life of faith, laying hold of the great and precious promises of God and looking definitely to Him in confidence for the full supply of all our needs. Remember, "Prayer changes things" and "Jesus NEVER fails." Thank God for the wonderful privilege we do have of having our lives enriched by this personal contact with the Heavenly Father, and by obedience and faith receiving the things we have need of.

In closing I earnestly pray that the experiences and testimonies given here may be an inspiration and a blessing to all who read them, and that the faith of many may be lifted up and strengthened. The God we serve is the LIVING God, He is loving, compassionate, tender, all-wise, and He desires the very best for His children. He has even promised that "the DESIRE of the righteous shall be granted," Prov. 10:24. Praise God! When we are truly His, living in vital touch with Him, our desires are purified and we want only what could be pleasing to Him, and then not one thing can hinder our getting prayer through. Let us love Him sincerely, live definitely for His glory, and go forth in the world shining out before others, with the blessed uplifting influence of "answered prayer" thrilling our hearts, and making us an inspiration and blessing to others.

Amen.

> "'Tis true, oh, yes, 'tis true
> God's wonderful promise is true;
> For I've trusted, and tested, and tried it,
> And I know God's promise is true."

Cooking For Christmas Dinner

AFTER A TORNADO STRUCK THE HOME

THIS FATHER HAD TO LEAVE HIS CHILDREN

WÉRE BROTHERS

141

WE ARE BROTHERS

ONE MAN BAND

Printed in Great Britain
by Amazon

22135881R00091